JEFF BEZOS

In His Own Words

Raphael Afil

IN THEIR OWN WORDS SERIES

ISBN: 9782923241630

Biography

Jeff Bezos was born on January 12, 1964, in Albuquerque, New Mexico, to Jacklyn Gise and Ted Jorgensen, his mother was then a 17 year old student. The marriage of his parents lasted about one year. After their divorce she married Miguel Bezos, a Cuban immigrant who studied at the University of Albuquerque.

Miguel Bezos legally adopted Jeff and the family moved to Houston, Texas, where Miguel became an engineer at Exxon.

As a child, Jeff spent his summers at his grandfather's Texas ranch, vaccinating cattle and fixing windmills. He attended Miami Palmetto Senior High School and later studied Computer Science at Princeton University where he received his B.Sc. degree in Electrical Engineering.

After graduation, he worked at several firms on Wall Street.

From 1988 to 1990, he was a product manager at Bankers Trust.

From 1990 to 1994, he joined D. E. Shaw & Co, a hedge fund, where he became the youngest Vice President. There, he met and married MacKenzie Tuttle in 1993, they have four children, three boys and one girl adopted from China.

Early in 1995, he foresaw the potential of the internet and e-commerce and founded Amazon.com, an online book store. He named it Amazon after the Amazon River in South America and also because the name begins with the letter A, the first letter of the alphabet.

Three years later Bezos took Amazon public with an initial public offering.

In 1998, he added the online sale of music, video and consumer goods.

In 1999, Jeff Bezos was named Time magazine's Person of the Year.

In 2004, he founded Blue Origin, an aerospace company.

In 2006, Amazon.com launched its video-on-demand service. Initially known as Amazon Unbox on TiVo, it was eventually rebranded as Amazon Instant Video.

In 2007, Amazon introduced a handheld electronic reading device the Kindle.

In 2010, he introduced the Kindle Fire a color touchscreen minitablet computer.

He later launched Amazon Studios and AWS, Amazon Web Services.

In 2013, he announced the purchase of The Washington Post for 250 million dollars.

Also in 2013, he introduced Amazon Prime.

Bezos had been eyeing the food delivery market, and in 2017 Amazon announced it had acquired the Whole Foods grocery chain for $13.7 billion in cash.

In early 2018, The Seattle Times reported that Amazon had consolidated its consumer retail operations in order to focus on growing areas including digital entertainment and Alexa, Amazon's virtual assistant.

Bezos premiered several original programs with the launch of Amazon Studios in 2013. The company hit it big in 2014 with the critically acclaimed Transparent and Mozart in the Jungle.

The initial success of the company was meteoric. With no press promotion, Amazon.com sold books across the United States and in 45 foreign countries within 30 days. In two months, sales reached $20,000 a week, growing faster than Bezos and his startup team had envisioned.

While many dot.coms of the early '90s went bust, Amazon flourished with yearly sales that jumped from $510,000 in 1995 to over $17 billion in 2011.

As part of the 2018 annual shareholder letter, Jeff Bezos said the company had surpassed 100 million paid subscribers for Amazon Prime. By September 2018, Amazon was valued at more than $1 trillion, the second company to ever hit that record just a few weeks after Apple.

In 1999, he was put on the cover of TIME magazine's Person of the Year.

In 2020, with annual revenue up 38% to $386 billion, a yearly increase of over $100 billion. Net profit for Amazon was up 84% for the year as compared to last year.

As of July 2021, Amazon has a market cap of $1.770 Trillion. This makes Amazon the world's 4th most valuable company by market cap in the world.

MacKenzie Bezos and Jeff Bezos divorced in July 2019, after 25 years of marriage.

A King County, Washington judge signed an order formalizing the separation that sets the stage for the transfer of some 19.7 million shares of Amazon.com Inc. to MacKenzie's name. That 4% holding valued at $38.3 billion, in 2019 is worth today in 2021, at about $60 billion.

Jeff Bezos has announced that he will be stepping down as the Chief Executive Officer (CEO) of the e-commerce giant in July 2021, handing over the reins of the company to Andy Jassy.

In a memo addressing all Amazon employees, Bezos said this move would allow him, "the time and energy I need to focus on the Day1 Fund, the Bezos Earth Fund, Blue Origin, The Washington Post, and my other passions".

Bezos will blast into space on July 20, 2021, when Blue Origin's New Shepard rocket makes its first flight with a crew, bringing along his younger brother Mark.

In July 2021, Bezos broke a new record becoming the first man in the world to be worth more than $200 billion.

Princeton Commencement Speech
(2010)

As a kid, I spent my summers with my grandparents on their ranch in Texas. I helped fix windmills, vaccinate cattle, and do other chores. We also watched soap operas every afternoon, especially Days of Our Lives. My grandparents belonged to a Caravan Club, a group of Airstream trailer owners who traveled together around the US and Canada and every few summers we'd join the caravan. We'd hitch up the Airstream to my grandfather's car and off we'd go and align with 300 other Airstream adventurers. I loved and worshiped my grandparents and I really looked forward to these trips.

On one particular trip I was about 10 years old, I was rolling around in the big bench seat in the back of the car. My grandfather was driving and my grandmother had the passenger seat. She smoked throughout these trips and I hated the smell. At that age, I'd take any excuse to make estimates and do minor arithmetic. I'd calculate our gas mileage, figure out useless statistics on things like grocery spending. I'd been hearing an ad campaign about smoking. I can't remember the details, but basically the ad said, "Every puff of a cigarette, take some number of minutes off of your life." I think it might've been two minutes per puff.

At any rate, I decided to do the math for my grandmother. I estimated the number of cigarettes per day, estimated the number of puffs per cigarette and so on. When I was satisfied that I'd come up with a reasonable number, I poked my head into the front of the car, tapped my grandmother on the shoulder and proudly proclaimed, "At two minutes per puff, you've taken nine years off of your life." I have a very vivid memory of what happened next, and it was not what I had expected. I expected to be applauded for my cleverness and my arithmetic skill. "Jeff, you're so smart. You had to have made some tricky estimates, figure out the number of minutes in a year and do some division." That's not what happened. Instead, my grandmother burst into tears.

I sat in the backseat. I Didn't know what to do while my grandmother was crying. My grandfather, who'd been driving in silence, pulled over onto the shoulder of the highway. He got out of the car and came around and opened my door and waited for me to follow. Was I in trouble? My grandfather was a highly intelligent, quiet man. He had never said a harsh word to me and maybe this was to be the first time. Or maybe he would ask that I get back in the car and apologize to my grandmother. I had no experience in this realm with my grandparents and no way to gauge what the consequences might be. We stopped beside the trailer. My grandfather looked at me and after a

bit of silence he gently and calmly said, "Jeff, one day you'll understand that it's harder to be kind than clever."
What I want to talk to you about today is the difference between gifts and choices. Cleverness is a gift. Kindness is a choice. Gifts are easy. They're given, after all. Choices can be hard. You can seduce yourself with your gifts if you're not careful. And if you do, it'll probably be to the detriment of your choices. This is a group with many gifts. I'm sure one of your gifts is the gift of a smart and capable brain. I'm confident that's the case because admission is competitive. And if there weren't some signs that you're clever, the Dean of Admissions wouldn't have let you in.

Your smarts will come in handy because you will travel in a land of marvels. We humans, plotting as we are, will astonish ourselves. We'll invent ways to generate clean energy and a lot of it. Atom by atom we'll assemble small machines that can enter cell walls and make repairs. This month comes the extraordinary but inevitable news that we've synthesized life. In the coming years we'll not only synthesize it, but engineer it to specifications. I believe you'll even see us understand the human brain. Jules Verne, Mark Twain, Galileo, Newton, all the curious from the ages would have wanted to be alive most of all right now. As a civilization, we will have so many gifts just as you as individuals have so many individual gifts as you sit before me. How will you use these gifts, and will you take pride in your gifts or pride in your choices?

I got the idea to start Amazon 16 years ago. I came across the fact that web usage was growing at 2300% per year and I'd never seen or heard of anything the grew that fast. The idea of building an online bookstore with millions of titles, something that simply couldn't exist in the physical world was very exciting to me. I had just turned 30 years old and I'd been married for a year. I told my wife MacKenzie that I wanted to quit my job and go do this crazy thing that probably wouldn't work since most startups don't and I wasn't sure what would happen after that. Mackenzie, also a Princeton grad and sitting here in the second row, told me I should go for it.

As a young boy, I had been a garage inventor. I'd invented an automatic gate closer out of cement filled tires, a solar cooker that didn't work very well out of an umbrella and aluminum foil, baking pan alarms to entrap my siblings. I'd always wanted to be an inventor and she wanted me to follow my passion. I was working at a financial firm in New York City with a bunch of very smart people and I had a brilliant boss I much admired. I went to my boss and told him I was going to start a company selling books on the internet. He took me on a long walk in Central Park, listened carefully to me and finally said, "That sounds like a really good idea, but it would be an even better idea for someone who didn't already have a good job." That logic made some sense to me and he convinced me to think about it for 48 hours before making a final decision. Seen in that light it really was a difficult choice, but ultimately I decided I had to give it a shot. I didn't think I'd regret trying and failing. And I suspected I would always be haunted by a decision to not try at all. After much consideration, I took the less safe path to follow my passion and I'm proud of that choice.

Tomorrow in a very real sense your life, the life you author from scratch on your own begins. How will you use your gifts? What choices will you make? Will inertia be your guide or will you follow your passions? Will you follow dogma or will you be original? Will you choose a life of ease or a life of service and adventure? Will you wilt under criticism or will you follow your convictions? Will you bluff it out when you're wrong or will you apologize? Will you guard your heart against rejection or will you act when you fall in love? Will you play it safe or will you be a little bit swashbuckling? When it's tough, will you give up or will you be relentless? Will you be a cynic or will you be a builder? Will you be clever at the expense of others or will you be kind?

I will hazard a prediction. When you are 80 years old and in a quiet moment of reflection, narrating for only yourself the most personal version of your life story, the telling that will be most compact and meaningful will be the series of choices you have made. In the end, we are our choices. Build yourself a great story. Thank you and good luck.

Interview with Charlie Rose

(2016)

Charlie Rose: Jeff Bezos founded Amazon in 1994 out of his garage as an online bookseller. Today, it is among the world's most valuable companies. He is one of the world's richest people, second only to Bill Gates. Amazon's ambition is to sell everything to everybody. Amazon's reach spans well beyond its retailing roots. Amazon Web Services is a leading company in the Cloud. In January, Amazon became the first digital streaming service to win a Golden Globe for best TV series. Jeff Bezos had many passions. He founded the aerospace company Blue Origin to lower the cost of space travel and increase its safety. In 2013, he purchased "The Washington Post." I met with him earlier today at the Economic Club here in New York. Here is that conversation. What is it that Amazon wants to be?

Jeff Bezos: Well, there are a couple of answers to that. Probably the biggest one, the best way, if I have to choose a single way to answer that question, is the thing that connects everything that Amazon does is the number one -- our number one conviction and idea and philosophy and principle which is customer obsession, as opposed to competitor obsession. And so we are always focused on the customer, working backwards from the customer's needs, developing new skills internally so that we can satisfy what we perceive to be future customer needs. We have a whole working backward process that starts with the customer needs and works backwards. So that is really, if you look at, seems like we are in a bunch of different businesses. So we have Amazon Web Services which is completely different from our, you know, Amazon Prime Business or Amazon Marketplace, or Amazon Studios, and so on. But really, the way that the businesses are run is very, very similar. And it all starts with, it's not just customer obsession, that is the number one. But we have a very inventive culture, so we like to pioneer invent.

There are other very effective business strategies. Pioneering is not the only effective business strategy. In fact, some people would argue it's not the most effective one. Close following can be a very good business strategy and it's worked many times if you look at the history of business. But it isn't who we are. Willingness to think long-term. I think that is another common thread that runs through every single thing we do. We are very happy to invest in new initiatives that are very risky, for five to seven years, which most companies won't do that. Companies will invest for very long periods of time, and they should in those cases where the outcomes are more certain. It's the combination of the risk-taking and the long-term outlook that make Amazon, not unique, but special in a smaller crowd. And then finally, taking real pride in operational excellence, so just doing things well, finding defects, and working backwards. That is all the incremental improvement that in business, most successful companies are very good at this one. If you are not good at finding defects, finding the root cause of the defects, fixing that root cause, you don't want to ever let defects flow downstream. That is a key part of doing a good job in any business, in my opinion.

Charlie Rose: You still want to sell everything to everybody.

Jeff Bezos: Yeah, for sure. We started, just remember, 20 years ago, we were selling only books. I was driving all the packages to the post office myself. I thought maybe one day we would be able to afford a forklift. And it is very, it's very, very different today. But we, over time, we added music and we added videos. And then I sent an email message out to the customer base, actually a thousand randomly selected customers, and I said, besides books, music and video, what would you like to see us sell? And the list came back incredibly long. It was basically just whatever the person had on their mind right now. One of our customers said, I wish you sold windshield wipers because I need windshield wipers for my car. A light kind of went on in my head. You know, people will want to use this new fangled e-commerce way of shopping for everything. Because people are very convenience-motivated. And if we can do it, so that really started the kind of the expansion into all categories, consumer electronics, and then apparel, and so on.

Charlie Rose: Take one example, apparel, you now have I think outpaced Macy's as the largest apparel seller in the world.

Jeff Bezos: Yeah, I don't know -- I've seen those headlines. I actually have not tried to track that. Back to not being competitor obsessed. But you know, we are selling a lot of apparel. And that team is doing a fantastic job. I do think, you know, if we're not the largest, we're among the largest apparel sellers in the world. And there is lots of room. You know, we keep improving. I think if you were to talk to our apparel team, they would tell you that they don't think we're very good at it yet. And still the business is going very well. So I am never disappointed when we're not good at something because I think, we'll think how good it's going to work when we are good at it. And the apparel is like that. There is so much opportunity. Nobody really knows how to do a great job of offering --apparel online yet. And we have tons of invention and ideas and working our way through that experimental list.

Charlie Rose: You have said that there are three pillars -- the Marketplace, Amazon Prime, and Amazon Web Services.

Jeff Bezos: That's right.

Charlie Rose: Let's go in reverse order. Amazon Web Services now is the largest contributor to revenue it is said.

Jeff Bezos: Well, not to revenue. It's a big contributor to profit. Our retail business, by the way, in our established countries, is also very profitable. We keep investing so we are investing in video, original content with Amazon Studios and so on. But

Amazon Web Services is a -- is remarkable I think for a couple of reasons. It follows all these principles that I laid out at the beginning. But one of the most unusual things that happened with Amazon Web Services is the amount of runway that we got, which is a gift, before we faced like-minded competition, we had -- it appears to me just empirically that if you invent a new way of doing something, typically if you are lucky, you get about two years of runway before competitors copy your idea. And two years is actually a pretty long time in a fast-moving industry so that's a big head start. For whatever reason, and I have a hypothesis of what the reason is. But for whatever reason, Amazon Web Services got seven years of runway before we faced like-minded competition.

There were other people doing similar kinds of things but not the same way and not with the same approach and same mindset. And in my experience, that's unheard of to get so much runway. And I think the reason that that happened is because the incumbents in technology for enterprises, sort of infrastructure technology for enterprises, thought that what we were doing was just so damn weird that it could never work. And so we just kept very quiet about it. And we knew it was working, you know, and we would read news stories that would say things like, do you really think anybody is going to buy a mission critical enterprise infrastructure from an online bookseller? And we would look at that, you know, and certain people were praying on that and we would read those articles and we would look at our business statement and we would be like, well, they are. So we kind of knew. But it was, so we got very lucky. That was a gift. And what that allowed us to do was build a gigantic advantage in terms of the feature set and the service offerings and the cost structure and everything else, that you just can't wave a magic wand and do that quickly. It takes years and years.

Charlie Rose: But the central point seemed to me --

Jeff Bezos: And now we're not stopping, so that team is, you know, every year, 500, 600, 700, 800 new features and services, so they keep pushing on that. That team is just doing an amazing job.

Charlie Rose: What's interesting to me is that you were doing it for yourself, these are things you were doing for yourself and you said, if we are you doing it for ourselves.

Jeff Bezos: This is true. So the founding idea behind Amazon Web Services is that our applications engineers and our networking and data center engineers were spending way too much time coordinating. And so the applications engineers are the ones who build the things that customers actually interact with, they drive the business forward, they drive revenues. Building data centers and building, you know, putting servers in the data centers and building fleets of servers and getting the right levels of capacity and making sure all the operating systems versions were correct and so on and so on. Databases on top of that, make sure the versions of those are correct, all the networking that goes with it. This stuff is unbelievably complicated and hard, every bit as hard as building the application layer. But it doesn't really add any value to the application layer. It's a kind of price of admission. It's one of those things that has to be done perfectly but it's not secret sauce. It's not going to change the way you run your business.

What we wanted to do was reduce those fine-grained conversations that the application engineers were having with the networking engineers. And so we said we should just create a set of APIs, application programming interfaces, harden those. And then the teams can discuss the road map next year, two years from now, three years from now. They can discuss in a course-grained way the road map of what APIs we should expose and then it will simplify those conversations and give a lot of stability and they won't need to do all these silly fine-grained coordination conversations. And so, we started designing that. And the second we started writing it down, we realized wait a second, what we're building here, we need. Amazon.com, the retailer needs these things. But pretty soon everybody is going to need these things. And so, with a little extra work, we can turn what we were going to build just for ourselves into a service for the world. And that's what we did. And it is now, you know, very successful.

Charlie Rose: The largest factor in the Cloud.

Jeff Bezos: By far.

Charlie Rose: And CIA and a lot of other clients come to you.

Jeff Bezos: Yes.

Charlie Rose: You also have a large shipping contingent within your own operation.

Jeff Bezos: Yes, we do.

Charlie Rose: And there are some --

Jeff Bezos: We do billions of packages a year and it takes a lot of logistics.

Charlie Rose: So you are getting into the shipping business.

Jeff Bezos: We have an A-plus team.

Charlie Rose: So is it the same model? Are you doing something and you are doing it well, and we say, we could do this for other people, so we're going to get into the shipping business?

Jeff Bezos: Not quite. It's a little bit different. Here we're really being driven by capacity needs, especially if you look at the holiday selling season. The fact of the matter is that we need all of the capacity that we can get from the established transportation providers like U.S. Postal Service and UPS. We will take all the capacity that they can give us. And I am just talking about the U.S. The same story is playing right around the world, the Royal Mail and Deutsche Post and so on. And then in addition to that, we need more capacity, especially at peak. Just in order to continue to grow our business. So, we have kind of been forced into developing expertise in the last mile. And of course, we do use it for our third-party business so third-party sellers can now use the Marketplace business. We offer a service called "Fulfilled by Amazon" where third-party sellers can put their inventory in our fulfillment centers. And then we handle all of the fulfillment and returns and customer service and everything else for them. And so we are, you know, that logistics chain is going to work for us, and for third-party sellers. And it's really crucial that we continue to build that out.

Charlie Rose: So, FedEx and UPS need not worry.

Jeff Bezos: No, no. If you look at those guys are going to be able to continue to grow and we're going to continue to grow with them, and just, and still need additional capacity.

Charlie Rose: The other thing is Amazon Prime, the second pillar, Amazon Prime, somewhat, 65 million members of Amazon Prime?

Jeff Bezos: We don't reveal that. So I don't want to nod.

Charlie Rose: Amazon is reasonably secretive.

Jeff Bezos: Well, we don't want to reveal things that will help competitors or alert them. And it's also just really hard to figure out which things would help them. You know, like we certainly got a bigger window, I was talking about our AWS business and how we got such a long runway. If we had been out there bragging about that business, we would have attracted attention from incumbents, much sooner than what actually happened. And so there is no reason in business usually to boast about your accomplishments. People will figure them out. Boasting about the number of Prime members won't make anybody more likely to join Prime, in my opinion. People already know that a lot of people are Prime members. Their friends are already Prime members. So it's true that in consumer businesses and in enterprise businesses that people, to some degree, like to be with the leader and like to be in the crowd. And so you do want people to know that you are a leader. You do want people to know that the offerings are successful and that lots of people are using them. But you don't have to quantity that for consumers or enterprises.

Charlie Rose: Let's assume it is a large number.

Jeff Bezos: It's a large number.

Charlie Rose: Why is it so crucial for your future Prime?

Jeff Bezos: Well, Prime is, what we want Prime to be and what we have developed it into over time is, it's the best of Amazon. So, you can get, basically if you join Prime, we want to have our core service be outstanding, and anybody who wants to use Amazon and not be a Prime member should have a great experience. And people who are not Prime members, for example, can still get free shipping. They have to buy a certain number of products or certain things to get above a certain product kind of order basket hurdle, I think it's $49. And if they get above that $49 hurdle, then they can get free shipping. And so what we did with Prime is say look, you know, you can get free shipping without joining Prime, but if you want fast free shipping, our best service, then you need to join Prime.

Charlie Rose: It's $99 a year.

Jeff Bezos: It's $99 a year. And then we started adding other benefits to it that we know that people like. So we started out -- we added Prime Video which has been a very successful new benefit for Prime. We started many years ago. We added just 10 or 20,000 shows. And they were all licensed and they were all reruns. Things like Gilligan's island. And it was kind of a by the way offering. So, you know, we said, look, you already are a Prime member, here is a new benefit. We know it's not the most important TV shows in the world, but it also isn't costing you anything extra. So, it grew. Now we're doing, you know, Emmy award-winning and Golden Globe award-winning original content that again, you get access to just at no additional charge, just being a Prime member.

Charlie Rose: So, getting into the creative part of the entertainment business, what was the motivation for that?

Jeff Bezos: Well, from a business point of view, there are two different ways to think about that. We always start with the customer-centric point of view. And then so how can we, if we're going to make original content which Amazon Studios is doing, how can it be better or different from the -- so much content that is out there that you could license already and not have to make yourself. And the fact of the matter is that the over the top streaming services with a subscription model can have -- can in fact make different kinds of content, so a show like "Transparent" which has won Golden Globes and Emmys is not ever -- it is not a show that could be successfully done on broadcast TV because broadcast TV needs a much bigger audience for that. "Transparent" -- we want to make shows that are somebody's favorite show. And on broadcast TV, you can be very happy if you have a big show that is, you know, 20 million people's third favorite show. And so you can actually think about the creative process a little differently. You can attract different storytellers. You can go for stories that are narrower but incredibly powerful and well told. "Mozart in the Jungle" is the same way. I don't see how "Mozart in the Jungle" another one that has won Golden Globes and Emmys, I don't see how it could be successful on broadcast TV either. So you get -- we can attract a storyteller who wants to tell a certain kind of story. Then there are other things that are just tailwinds in this business, that are happening because of HBO and Netflix and others that, you know, ten years ago, you couldn't get A List Talent to do TV. They perceived it as stigmatizing.And today that is just completely not. Today, A List Talent wants to do serialized TV Because the quality of the storytelling is so high that it's just completely flipped on its head.

Charlie Rose: Does it benefit your traditional e-commerce businesses? The fact that you have a presence in entertainment and the fact that you went --

Jeff Bezos: Totally.

Charlie Rose: You sell things because you win awards in Hollywood.

Jeff Bezos: There is the customer experience part of -- you know, we want storytellers with guts and taste to do things that are somebody's favorite show. And then let's talk about the business side of that. Why these shows are expensive? Man in the High Castle, which is our most watched and one of our highest rated shows, and you should watch it if you haven't seen it, Hitler won World War II, it's an alternative history, and it's 1962, and the Nazis control the east coast and the Japanese control the West Coast. It's creepy. And but that show is super expensive to make. And so how do you pay for that content? That's the business side of this.

Charlie Rose: Right.

Jeff Bezos: The business side is very unique to Amazon. I don't think there's another model out there like it. And that is when you become a Prime member, you buy more from us. You say to yourself, well, what else -- now that I have paid my $99 a year, how else can I use this membership? And so when people join Prime, they buy more shoes, they buy more diapers, they buy more dishwashing detergent, they buy more books and electronics and toys and so on and so on. And so we really want people to join Prime. And we really want people to renew their Prime membership. And so when we make, when we win a Golden Globe, for us, what we are tying that too, and we can see -- we can see this in the metrics that people who use Prime Video are more likely to convert from free trial lists to paid Prime members and are more likely to convert from paid Prime members, their next time, not convert but to renew for a subsequent year. And so that's what closes the loop on the business side. You don't do things for business reasons. You need to do things for the customer experience reasons. But you need to know how you are going to pay for that customer experience. You need to close the loop on the business side too.

Charlie Rose: So I have listed three pillars. What might be the fourth pillar?

Jeff Bezos: Well, it could be, we don't know yet is the real answer. And I think it's very hard to -- we do a lot of different things. And these things, the fourth one will rise and distinguish itself. We'll put energy into many things. I'm optimistic about things like Amazon Studios, so the original content, I think that actually could become a fourth pillar on its own. And I think that what we are doing with natural language understanding and Echo and Alexa could become a fourth pillar.

Charlie Rose: Everybody talks about artificial intelligence and everybody is investing.

Jeff Bezos: And by the way, rightly so, this is the real thing.

Charlie Rose: Enlarge on that and also on the idea of what Echo is and how it may very well be the beginning on the edge, the wedge into artificial intelligence, that benefits everybody.

Jeff Bezos: Well, Echo is a small black cylinder that is -- it has seven microphones on the top and has a speaker inside and a digital signal processor and some other computer inside. It's WiFi-connected to the Cloud. And Alexa, the agent -- the artificially intelligent agent that lives in the Cloud will talk to you through Alexa -- through Echo. And one of the interesting things about Echo, the device, is it uses those seven microphones to do something called beam forming. And so basically it can hear you very well even in a very loud kitchen environment. For example, you have the dishwasher running and you have the sink running water and maybe somebody is playing the television set in the living room. And Alexa can still hear you because of that digital signal processing. And so you can say, Alexa, what time is it? Alexa, what is the weather today? Alexa, and in natural language, Alexa, play a certain song, et cetera, et cetera. And people really -- it's just been a big hit. We launched it a few years ago. It has vastly exceeded our expectations in terms of volume. We have literally thousands of people dedicated to working on it.

Charlie Rose: And Google wants to be in that business and everybody else wants to be in that business.

Jeff Bezos: Everybody will want to be in that business. And so here you know we got the kind of standard, you know, two, two-and-a-half-year head start.

Charlie Rose: Let me talk about "The Washington Post."

Jeff Bezos: Yeah.

Charlie Rose: You bought "The Washington Post" without doing any due diligence. You were so impressed with --

Jeff Bezos: Well, I did no due diligence because I knew Don Graham for 15 years.

Charlie Rose: Did he come to you because he needed a --

Jeff Bezos: If any of you know Don Graham, he is possibly the most honorable person in the world. So, he just laid out all the warts for me. He laid out all of the great things about "The Post" for me. And no amount of due diligence could ever have gotten to more clarity than just talking to Don for several hours.

Charlie Rose: Why did you buy it?

Jeff Bezos: I bought it because it's important. So, I would never buy a financially upside down salty snack food company. You know, that doesn't make any sense to me. But "The Washington Post" is important. And so, it makes sense to me to take something like that, and I also am optimistic. And I thought there were some ways to make it -- I want it to be a self-sustaining, profitable enterprise. I think that would be healthy for "The Post." And I think it can be done. And our approach is actually very, very simple. We need to go -- it's hard to execute on and it will take time but the approach is simple. We need to go from making a relatively large amount of money per reader on a relatively small number of readers. That is the historic model of "The Post," to a model where we make a relatively small amount of money per reader on a very large number of readers. That is the new model.

Charlie Rose: But that's your business model too, isn't it?

Jeff Bezos: That is the better business model for the internet era. And the Post is unusual, and this is one of the things from a business point of view why I'm so optimistic about The Post, is that it can go from, it has historically been a local paper. A very good local paper. But it happens to be a local paper situated in the capital city of the United States of America. And it's kind of geographic location is superb for converting it from being a local paper to a national and even a global publication. And so that, and that's a gift that the internet brings. To do national and global publication in the days of print, super expensive. You have to figure out how to have printing presses everywhere and distribution everywhere, physical distribution, very challenging. Today, that piece is easy. To get global distribution in digital form is extraordinarily simple.

Charlie Rose: Because it is an important newspaper in the nation's capital and most powerful country in the world, did you want it also because it would give you political influence?

Jeff Bezos: No. And I think one of the reasons that Don Graham liked me as an owner is because he didn't think I would politicize it.

Charlie Rose: Yeah.

Jeff Bezos: And so, you know, I think because it is in the capital city of the United States of America, it should not be, you know, you take the British model of newspapers and, you know, the kind of left-wing paper or right-wing paper. And there are certain people who if they had bought "The Washington Post" would have converted it in one of those directions. And I don't think that would be healthy for "The Post" or healthy for the country and plus in that respect, I'm also a good owner because I'm so damn busy. Honestly.

Charlie Rose: You're not hanging out in the newsroom.

Jeff Bezos: I have no desire to meddle. I have no desire to opine on everything. I can't -- I don't have the time to be in the newsroom every day or even for the editorial pages. And, by the way, it's a very difficult business that needs to be done by professionals. I sometimes get asked, you know, do you opine in the newsroom or get involved in newsroom activities. I'm like, if you know as I do know a little bit about newsrooms, you will see, it would be exactly the equivalent of me walking into a surgical theater while my son was having brain surgery and meddling with the brain surgeon. It doesn't make sense. These are super complex -- being the executive editor of "The Post," we have Marty Baron who, in my opinion, is the best executive editor in the world. He and his team, they are doing an unbelievably good job. And again, back to, you know, I have been talking about the business model of "The Post" we had to transition into this new way of having a small amount of money with lots of readers. The real reason this could work is because "The Post" is creating riveting coverage, and they're doing it. They are -- you can't, you know, turn around a restaurant with business techniques if the food isn't delicious. And we have delicious content, you know, "The Post" is just riveting, they are killing it. I am so proud of that team.

Charlie Rose: People in my profession are great admirers of what "The Washington Post" is today under Marty Baron's leadership.

Jeff Bezos: Totally.

Charlie Rose: Especially in foreign coverage.

Jeff Bezos: Yes. And by the way, Marty would be the first one to tell you this, it is his team, I mean, he put those people in place and he has given them lots of kind of energy and they're proud of the product they're creating. "The Post" also has a culture that -- I also have no desire to change the culture of The Post, that would be so counterproductive. They already have a great culture and it comes all the way -- you know it is decades old. What you want to do with something like "The Post" that has a very healthy decades-old culture is instead of trying to change it, you want to kind of uncover it and reveal it and burnish it. And the more I've gotten to know about "The Post," I realize the distinguishing feature of "The Post" compared to some other very high-quality newspapers is "The Post" has more swagger. They are, they are swashbuckling, but they are professional swashbucklers which is very important because non-professional swashbuckling just gets you killed. You know, you can't do that, and they are just incredible.

Charlie Rose: Blue Origin. You and I sat last night with a former astronaut.

Jeff Bezos: That was very fun, Scott Kelly.

Charlie Rose: Scott Kelly who was there at the International Space Station for, I don't know how many days. What is it that you hope to accomplish?

Jeff Bezos: In space.

Charlie Rose: In space.

Jeff Bezos: Well, this is, first of all, let's back up. This is a childhood dream. I fell in love with the idea of space and space exploration and space travel when I was five years old. I watched Neil Armstrong step onto the moon. You don't choose your passions, your passions choose you. I -- so I am infected with this idea. I couldn't ever stop thinking about space. I have been thinking about it ever since then. And I just -- so again, you know, I did not, when I started Blue Origin, which is the name of this space company, I did not make a list of all the businesses in the world where I thought I might get the highest return on invested capital. And it was driven by passion and curiosity and the need to explore the things that I care about. And so we have, over time, built a brilliant team, there are now over 800 people at Blue Origin, we have a suborbital tourism vehicle called "New Shepherd" that flies like a regular rocket when it launches and then lands on its tail like a Buck Rogers rocket. We have used the same vehicle, it is reusable. We used the same vehicle five times --

Charlie Rose: And that's key to the business of going into space.

Jeff Bezos: That's the absolute key. If you look -- if you ask the question, why is space travel so expensive? There is one reason, and it's because we throw the hardware away every time after using it. It is all expendable. And even in the past when we have done things that were sort of semi-reusable, they weren't really what I would call operable reusability because they were disassembled, inspected and then put back together. So you can imagine how expensive air travel would be if, after your Hawaii vacation, you get to Hawaii and -- well, if they throw the 747 away, it is going to be really expensive but it is also going to be super expensive if, after you get to Hawaii, they disassemble the whole thing, inspect every part and put it all back together before you're allowed to fly again.

That was the problem with the space shuttle. And so, it is really important that you design the vehicle from the beginning for highly operable reusability. The propellants are incredibly low cost. People don't know this about rockets, but a big rocket, let's say, has a million pounds of propellant on board, two thirds of that may be liquid oxygen, say 600,000 pounds or so of liquid oxygen. Do you know how much liquid oxygen costs? Ten cents a pound. So, that is $60,000 worth of liquid oxygen, and then add the fuel costs in. You are still talking about a few hundred thousand dollars in propellant costs. And the launch, you know, costs on the order of $60 million, $70 million, $80 million, $100 million, $150 million. So how do you get from a $100 million -- $100 million to $300,000 of propellants -- it's simple, you are throwing the hardware away. And so it's really not -- the engineering challenge involved in building a highly operable reusable vehicle is gigantic. But if you can do that, it is a game changer. You change everything. And now why -- to your original question. That is sort of the background. I believe it's incredibly important that we humans go out into space and the primary reason, if you think long-term about this, is we need to do that to preserve the earth. So I am not -- I'm not one of the Plan B guys.

There is a conventional -- there is a kind of conventional wisdom that is quite common that one of the reasons we need to go into space and settle another planet is as a kind of backup for humanity, you know, if earth gets destroyed, at least we have this other place. And I don't like that -- that's not motivating for me. But what -- because I'll tell you what we know for sure. We have now sent robotic probes to every planet in this solar system. We have taken close looks at them all, and believe me, this is the best planet, It is not even close. So, what you need to do, and if you look at -- if you want a thriving, growing civilization, you want population growth to continue, you want a whole bunch of things to continue. And I believe that in the next few hundred years, what will happen is we will move all heavy industry into space for a whole bunch of practical reasons, easier access to resources of all kinds, material resources as well as energy. If you think about solar energy on Earth, it is inherently problematic because it only is available half the time. In space, solar energy is available 24/7. But the list of practical reasons why that --

Charlie Rose: But you also have to build an infrastructure up there.

Jeff Bezos: Yeah, and that's why you need really low cost. You need to shrink the cost of lifting mass into space from Earth by two orders of magnitude. You need to reduce that cost by a hundred times and then you can do these things. And then Blue Origin is not going to do this all by ourselves. What I want to do with Blue Origin is build heavy-lifting infrastructure that lowers the cost of access to space so that the next generation of entrepreneurs can have a dynamic entrepreneurial explosion in space. That is how we will move all heavy industry into space and then ultimately Earth can be effectively zoned, residential and light industrial.

Charlie Rose: Finally, and unlike the internet there was infrastructure there, so when you jumped into the internet there was always infrastructure there.

Jeff Bezos: This is the key point, when entrepreneurs -- so Amazon was a tiny, little company that started with four people, and that -- we could only do, we built Amazon because we didn't have to do any of the heavy lifting. The transportation and logistics infrastructure of U.S. Postal Service which would have been hundreds of billions in CapEx, already existed. We didn't have to build the internet, it was run on, on long-distance cables that were actually put in the ground for long-distance phone calls. And we didn't have to build a payment system, the credit card system already existed. So all these things would have been tens of billions or hundreds of billions in CapEx and we got to rest on top of them. That's why you don't see entrepreneurial dynamism in space like you do on the internet. On the internet, two kids in a dorm room can take, change an industry completely, and you can't do that in space. The price of admission is too high. Because the -- just getting to space is so expensive. And so if we can change, if I'm 80 years old, looking back on my life and the one thing I have done is make it so that there is this gigantic entrepreneurial explosion in space for the next generation, I will be a happy, happy man.

Charlie Rose: OK, one other thing I want to say before we go and the last question, you and Bill Gates got together and started something called Grail, a company fighting cancer.

Jeff Bezos: Yes.

Charlie Rose: And the idea is?

Jeff Bezos: The science of that is unbelievable. And basically, you can sequence -- tumors shed little bits of DNA into your bloodstream. And you can use sequencing technology to amplify those things and then detect cancers at very, very early stages. And for a lot of cancers early detection is a big deal. So this is -- the science of this is very promising, very real, and it might not work. But it might. And I'm optimistic.

Charlie Rose: The market cap --

Jeff Bezos: If it does work, it's a big, big deal.

Charlie Rose: The market cap of Amazon has made you the second wealthiest person in the world. Second to Bill Gates. Can you imagine at some point in your life pursuing the kind of philanthropy?

Jeff Bezos: Well, yeah. If there is anything left after I finish building Blue Origin. We'll see. I did not choose Blue Origin based on -- you know, basically what I am doing right now is taking my Amazon winnings and investing them. Every time you see me sell stock on Amazon, it's sends more money to the Blue Origin team.

Charlie Rose: I asked Jeff last night at the Natural Museum of History, what was the return on investment for Blue Origin, and he said to me as he slapped me, that is a rude question.

Jeff Bezos: That is a very rude question. And, by the way, I do believe that Blue Origin can be a sustainable, profitable enterprise one day. But that is an investment horizon that would make most reasonable investors sick to their stomach.

Charlie Rose: By 2018, somebody will be up on a vessel.

Jeff Bezos: Yeah. We are on track on our suborbital vehicle "New Shepherd" to fly paying passengers, hopefully in 2018. I keep telling the team, it's not a race. We'll do it when it's safe. But we're on track right now for 2018.

Charlie Rose: On behalf of everybody in this room, and the Economic Club of New York, thank you, Jeff Bezos.

Jeff Bezos: Thank you, Charlie.

Harvard Business Review

Adi Ignatius: Welcome to the HBR IdeaCast from Harvard Business Review. I'm Adi Ignatius, the editor in chief, and recently I talked to Amazon's Jeff Bezos, who in our new survey, which appears in the January issue, comes out as the world's number one living CEO. Here are excerpts of our conversation.

Jeff, thanks for joining us. When Amazon went public back in 1997, you wrote a letter to shareholders that said it's all about the long-term. Did you feel at the time that you were really challenging orthodoxy?

Jeff Bezos: I felt that we were trying to make sure that we were correctly advertising the actual event. Warren Buffett has a really good phrase for this. He says, "You can hold a rock concert, and that's OK. You can hold a ballet, and that's OK. Just don't hold a rock concert and advertise it as a ballet." The job of a public company is to be clear about whether you're holding a ballet or a rock concert, and then investors can opt into that.

Adi Ignatius: So what does it really mean from the perspective of a CEO to think in the long term?

Jeff Bezos: Well, if you're long-term oriented, customer interests and shareholder interests are aligned. In the short term, that's not always correct.

Also, we like to invent and do new things, and I know for sure that long-term orientation is essential for invention because you're going to have a lot of failures along the way.

Adi Ignatius: Jeff, you've said that you like to plant seeds that may take seven years to bear fruit. Doesn't that mean you'll lose some battles along the way to companies that have a more conventional two or three-year outlook?

Jeff Bezos: Well, maybe so, but I think some of the things that we have undertaken I think could not be done in two to three years. And so, basically if we needed to see meaningful financial results in two to three years, some of the most meaningful things we've done we would never have even started. Things like Kindle, things like Amazon Web Services, Amazon Prime. The list of such things is long at Amazon.

Adi Ignatius: So how much do you care about your share price?

Jeff Bezos: I care very much about our share owners, and so I care very much about our long-term share price. I do not follow the stock on a daily basis, and I don't think there's any the information in it. Benjamin Graham said, "In the short term, the stock market is a voting machine. In the long term, it's a weighing machine." And we try to build a company that wants to be weighed and not voted upon.

Adi Ignatius: So does it make sense for Amazon to even stay in the hardware business, which is low margin and low profit for you?

Jeff Bezos: Well, our approach to our hardware Kindle devices, Kindle Fire and our Kindle readers, is to sell the hardware at near break even, and then we have an ongoing relationship with the customer where they buy content from us, digital books, music, movies, TV shows, games, apps. And the reason that we like that approach is because we don't make $100 every time we sell a Kindle Fire HD, since it's near break even. Instead of making a bunch of money, we're happy if people keep using our products. We don't have to have you on the upgrade treadmill.

Adi Ignatius: You've said that you would be interested, if you had the right concept and approach, in creating a physical Amazon retail experience. Why even consider that?

Jeff Bezos: Well, we like to build innovative things. We'll look around the world, and we'll be inspired by what we see. But we like to put our own unique twist on it and do something that's not redundant. If there are 100, physical stores that are doing a great job, we don't want to be the 101st. If we can find something that we think customers would like that would be differentiated, it would be super fun to do that.

Adi Ignatius: So would developing a phone also fall into that innovative category?

Jeff Bezos: Yeah, absolutely. That's the kind of thing where you would ask what is the idea? How would it be differentiated? Why wouldn't it be me too?

Adi Ignatius: So do you fear is your biggest challenge?

Jeff Bezos: Well, we don't get up every morning thinking about what's the list of the top three companies that are going to try to kill us. I do know of companies, and their annual planning process starts with the list of their three top enemies, and they work from there. They get motivation from the competitive zeal. Our approach is not to start with that list. We do look at other companies, and so we pay attention, but it's not where we get our energy form.

Adi Ignatius: So disruption is obviously a rough business. Do you have any personal regrets about the pain that your success has caused to traditional retailers?

Jeff Bezos: I'm just as sentimental as the next person I have lots of childhood memories of physical books and things like that. Our job at Amazon is to build the best customer experience we can in every way and then let customers choose where they shop.

Adi Ignatius: At what point will the goal change from lowering margins, building market share, to making a bigger profit?

Jeff Bezos: Percentage margins are not one of the things we are seeking to optimize. It's the absolute dollar-free cash flow per share that you want to maximize, and if you can do that by lowering margins, we would do that. So if you could take the free cash flow, that's something that investors can spend. Investors can't spend percentage margins.

Adi Ignatius: Amazon has done a great job of self-cannibalizing its revenue streams, going from Amazon Store to Amazon Marketplace, from print to ebooks, and so on. In most companies, moves like those would be hard to execute without organizational turmoil. How have you managed the transitions?

Jeff Bezos: When things get complicated, we simplify by saying what's best for the customer? And then we take it as an article of faith if we do that, it'll work out the long-term. So we can never prove that. In fact, sometimes we've done a price elasticity studies, and the answer is always we should raise prices. And we don't do that because we believe– and again, we have to take this as an article of faith– we believe by keeping our prices very, very low, we earn trust with customers over time, and that that actually does maximize free cash flow over the long term.

Adi Ignatius: What have you learned about leadership from running what has become a very big company?

Jeff Bezos: Well, I would say one thing that I have learned within the first couple of years of starting the company is that in inventing and pioneering requires a willingness to be misunderstood for long periods of time. One of the early examples of this was the customer reviews. One wrote to me and said, "You don't understand your business. You make money when you sell things. Why do you allow these negative customer reviews?" And when I read that letter, I thought, we don't make money when we sell things. We make money when we help customers make purchase decisions.

Adi Ignatius: How do you institutionalize the ability to come up with these good, misunderstood ideas?

Jeff Bezos: Well, I think it's a couple of things. One is we have a lot of internal stories that we tell ourselves about persistence and patience, long-term thinking, staying heads down, focused on the customer even while being criticized. The second is selection of the people. When they wake up and are thinking in the shower in the morning, they're thinking about customers, and thinking about how to invent on behalf of customers, and they find that fun. And if you get here, and you find that you get your motivation from having a more competitive-focused culture, you might find our culture dull. We don't. We find a culture intensely fun.

Some companies, if you wanted to put it into a single word, they have a conqueror mentality, and we have an explorer mentality. And the people who like our mentality of exploration and pioneering, they tend to stay here, and have fun here, and that's self-reinforcing.

Adi Ignatius: You generated a lot of attention recently. Is all this publicity good for you and for Amazon.

Jeff Bezos: I have to be very choosy, and I've done less and less of it over time. And the reason that I'm doing this interview with you is I want customers to understand what makes us tick, how we operate, what our principles are. I think customers want to know who they're doing business with.

Adi Ignatius: Well, if you don't talk, how in the world can we misunderstand you?

Jeff Bezos: Believe me, that wouldn't stop it.

Business Insider's Talk

Few big successes compensate for dozens and dozens of things that didn't work. So, bold bets, AWS, Kindle, Amazon Prime, our third-party seller business, all of those things are examples of bold bets that did work, and they pay for a lot of experiments. I've made billions of dollars of failures at amazon.com, literally billions of dollars of failures. You might remember pets.com or Cosmo, or Give myself a root canal with no anesthesia very easily. None of those things are fun, but they don't matter. Part and parcel with ownership is a mentality of long term thinking. Owners think longer term than renters do.

I have a friend who rented his house to some tenants and instead of getting a Christmas tree stand at Christmas, they just nailed the Christmas tree into the hardwood floors of the house. No owner would ever do that, and sometimes that's a bad tenant. You know there are good tenants, but that's a bad tenant. It's because this is the same old thing about nobody ever washed a rental car. You take better care of the things that you own, but one of the responsibilities of ownership and definitely deep inside the Amazon culture, is to think about the fundamentals of the business and not the daily fluctuations in the stock price. There's no information in it, my main job today is, I work hard at helping to maintain the culture. A culture of high standards of operational excellence of inventiveness of willingness to fail, willingness to make a bold experiment.

I'm the guy, I'm the counterbalance to the institutional no, who can say yes. But I'm not going to be here forever, many of the traits that make Amazon unusual are now deeply ingrained in the culture. In fact, if I wanted to change them I couldn't. If I decided tomorrow that I wish Amazon did less pioneering and closer following, I couldn't do it. The cultures are self-reinforcing and that's a good thing. We get sometimes people come to the company and they find Amazon very boring, because we don't have enough competitive zeal. Some annual planning processes in some companies literally start with who are our three biggest enemies. Then here's how we're going to hold them at bay or defeat them. We don't have such a list at Amazon, it's not how our annual planning process works.

But on the other hand, if you're the kind of person who gets up in the morning and says in the shower time what can we invent for customers? What can we do differently and how can we improve that experience and so on, then you know it's going to be a playground. I still run into work by the way, if you want to do more of something, make the frictionless. If you want to do less of something, make the friction more. If there's a particular snack food that you like a lot and it's making you fat, put it on the top shelf where it's harder to get to and you'll eat less of it. Don't leave it on your kitchen counter. Business is very situational, so rules of thumb are good, but they have to be applied to the right situation.

Sometimes the old maxim that you should stick to the knitting is correct. But sometimes the adage that you should stick to the knitting is wrong and a senior leader's job is to figure out in which situation you are. I always tell our most senior executives at Amazon because you're a senior executive you have more control over your environment, and you should have less stress. If senior executives are saying they're so stressed out, I tell them look, you shouldn't be stressed out. Stress comes from a lack of control and because you're a senior exec, you have more control of your environment. Figure out what it is that's causing you stress and figure out how to do less of it. Bring somebody on your team who's good at that, or who likes doing it and have them shore you up in that regard.

I'm focusing on those things that I think make Amazon unusual. Genuine customer obsession, so like every single thing you just mentioned. When our senior executives sit down and review those programs, they're looking for customer obsession. Second one that we're focused on is invention. We don't like to do me too offerings, we'll be inspired by something we see in the world. We're not hermetically sealed, but we want to put our own twist on it. We want to try to do something better for customers, that's pioneering. So where's the invention? Why is this going to be better for customers than whatever is serving that need in the world today? And then a willingness to think long-term.

I'm very focused on those things and also the operational excellence, reducing defects at their root. Those are the things, that's the culture of Amazon. It's the habits that we have, those are the things I'm focused on. Those are the things that all of our senior people are focused on. They've been at the company for a long time and I'm incredibly lucky because I get to work with what are effectively paid volunteers. The senior team at Amazon most of them have been in the company for 10 plus years and they've ridden the stock appreciation of Amazon. They can all go sip a Pina Coladas on a beach for the rest of their life if they want to. I'm very grateful to them they choose not to, they do it because it's fun and we're building things.

We have so many talented people and the common thread in all of those things is our approach. You know I would definitely advise a small startup company to be as narrow and as focused as possible to be. If you look at the original Amazon business plan, there was no hint of anything other than books in it and it was not on my radar. I was thinking I wanted to build an online bookstore, that was it. It worked way better than I thought it would, we launched music and that worked better than I thought it would. We launched videos, it's so long ago I can't really remember. I think it was actually VHS tapes, is that possible? And that worked better than we thought it would.

Then I sent email to customers. I picked about a thousand customers, and I said beside the things we sell today, books, music, and video, what would you like to see us sell? The list came back incredibly long tail, it was almost like whatever was on their mind at the moment. It was like, I wish you sold windshield wipers for my car, and I was like really? Windshield wipers? That wasn't on the business plan, but that's an interesting idea. Today, if you're buying your windshield wipers anywhere else, you're probably getting ripped off. It's been kind of one foot in front of the other and then sometimes we expand into new areas in two ways. One is kind of from a customer need, we will work from a customer need to the skills that we need. The other one is skills forward from a skillset we have to a new set of customers.

Kindle is an example of a customer need and we don't have any hardware skills. We're doing this for 10 years now, but if you go back 10 years, we had no hardware team. We had to hire somebody to lead our hardware group and then build a hardware routine and build some institutional competence at it. That's a customer need backwards approach and in skills forward, a great example of that is Amazon Web Services. We had the skills to do AWS, we had probably more distributed computing expertise than anybody else in the world, because of the transactions. Transaction systems are so complicated and hard to build, we had a service-oriented architecture of great complexity, probably before anybody else. Because we were doing that, we could kind of see the future a little bit and decided to build AWS, which has turned into a huge business on its own.

Again my job, one of my jobs as the leader of Amazon is to encourage people to be bold and people love to focus on things that aren't yet working. That's good, it's human nature, that kind of divine discontent can be very helpful. But it's incredibly hard to get people to take bold bets and you need to encourage that. If you're going to take bold bets, they're going to be experiments and if they're experiments, you don't know ahead of time whether they're going to work. Experiments are by their very nature prone to failure, but big successes, a few big successes compensate for dozens and dozens of things that didn't work. Warren Buffet has this great quote, he says, you can hold a rock concert and that's okay. You can hold a ballet and that's okay. Just don't hold a rock concert and advertise it as a ballet.

Investors come in all shapes and sizes: they have different investment horizons, different approaches, different beliefs about what the right kind of portfolio looks like. So, people use Wall Street as a shorthand, but there isn't one type of investor. You have to be super clear about what kind of company you're trying to build, what your approach is. We laid that out in our 1997 annual shareholder letter, we said we were going to take big bets. We said they were going to fail, we said some of them, hopefully are going to work. We said we were going to invest for the long-term, that we were going to try to take advantage of market opportunities as they arose. There's a certain kind of investor who is aligned with that approach and so again, you can hold the ballet or the rock concert and both can work. But just be clear about which one you are, and then people can self-select.

Gala 2017, Jeff Bezos Fireside Chat

Michael Beckerman: My wife pointed out that one of things she loves about Amazon is you can look back at your purchases.

Jeff Bezos: Yes.

Michael Beckerman: It's a really great reflection of what's going on in your life at the time based on what you're buying. It occurred to me that the reverse is also true, that the e commerce journey that everybody probably in this room has gone on, mirrors what you and Amazon have gone through first. Only selling books and now selling everything is we've all kind of gone on that journey together. I looked back at my purchase history and in 2004, I bought exactly one thing on Amazon was a book. By 2006, I had a 500% increase in purchases: four books and one Gillette razor, which I used tonight.

Jeff Bezos: Hopefully a new one.

Michael Beckerman: The new one.

Jeff Bezos: Yes.

Michael Beckerman: Then by 2015 a year, we had just gotten married, moved into a home, got dogs. We bought everything for our dogs, we bought a TV, bought a snowblower, bought allergy medicine, peanut butter. I look these things up, literally everything, four days a week ordering. So, the question is, at what point did you realize you'd have the scale of success with

Amazon going from books to where you are now as a company?

Jeff Bezos: Well, I have a question for you, in 2004, do you know what book it was you bought?

Michael Beckerman: I do remember, it was writing screenplays that sell? And it did not?

Jeff Bezos: So how did that work out? That, like you want your money back?

Michael Beckerman: I could, I could even return?

Jeff Bezos: I'll take it back.

Michael Beckerman: Because that did not work for me. I'm going to keep my day job.

Jeff Bezos: But your question is, did I kind of anticipate what would happen over the last 22 years at Amazon? The answer is God no! So you know, Amazon started as a very small company. It was me and a few other people. I was driving all the packages to the post office myself in my 1987 Chevy Blazer. When I raised money for Amazon, I had to raise a million dollars, which I raised from 22 different investors $50,000 each. They got 20% of the company for the million dollars. Forty people told me no, so I had to take 60 meetings to get 20 yeses, the first question was always what's the internet? I had to walk through that, and this was 1994, early 95. So, did I anticipate, you know fast forward to today and the current version of it? No. It has been one foot in front of the other and I think that that is true for most businesses, where you kind of proceed adaptively. Its step by step, you figure it out. You have a success and then you kind of double down on that success. You figure out what else you can do, what customers want. Everything we've done and all the success we have is at its root primarily due to the fact that we have put customers first.

Michael Beckerman: So those few people are probably kicking themselves now.

Jeff Bezos: Well, it's very interesting, the 40 people who did not invest, it's kind of a study in human nature. I'm in touch with a few of them still and some of them take it in great stride and they recognize that they actually have ridiculously happy lives. Others of them actually cannot talk about it, it is actually just too painful. That's human nature and some people are better at rolling with the punches.

Michael Beckerman: I would be in the do not talk about it camp probably. But speaking of talking, I have the privilege of being able to talk to a lot of people in Washington about all of our member companies. Amazon is one where I think people have a very different idea of what Amazon is. Some people see you as an e commerce company or retailer, others see you as an innovative tech company. You have Amazon Web Services, you have original content, you have Alexa and so many other things. How should we be thinking about Amazon?

Jeff Bezos: Yes, I do get that. That is something that people get confused about sometimes, what is Amazon? We do such a diverse array of things, from producing original content at

Amazon Studios, to Amazon Web Services, where we sell startups and enterprises, computing infrastructure. To the things that most people know about, which is our consumer offering, where we deliver things in little brown boxes. These things seem so disparate, how is it that we're doing all of them? The common thread, and really what it is, is it's an approach. We have a very distinctive approach that we have been honing and refining and thinking about for 22 years. It's really just a few principles that we use as we go about these activities.

At the very top of the list is one I've already mentioned, but you'll probably hear it 10 times throughout tonight, because it's so central, and it is customer obsession. It's customer obsession instead of, for example, competitor obsession, or business model obsession, or product obsession, or technology obsession. There are many ways to center a business and by the way, many of them can work. I know and have friends who lead very competitor obsessed companies. Those companies can be successful. You know that's not a bad strategy, you have to be really good at close following. You identify winners when you watch your competitors very carefully. If they latch on to something that's working, you duplicate it as quickly as possible.

It's a very good strategy in some ways, because you don't have to go down blind alleys, if you're not pioneering, if you're only close following. It has some advantages, but it has some disadvantages too. I like the customer obsession model, I think it's the right one, I think it's better than product obsession, product recession is not bad, but I think customer obsession gets you there in a healthier way. So that's one of the principles, one of the approaches that we take in every single thing that we do. The second one is that we are willing, I would say even eager to invent and pioneer. I think that goes along, marries really well with customer obsession. Customers are always dissatisfied, even when they don't know it, even when they think they're happy. They actually do want a better way and they just don't know yet what that should be.

That's why I always warn people customer obsession is not just listening to customers. Customer obsession is also inventing on their behalf, because it's not their job to invent for themselves. So, you need to be an inventor and a pioneer. The third one that's really central to the way we think about all of our business problems and a bunch of things that Amazon, is we're long-term oriented. So I ask everybody to not think in two to three-year timeframes, but to think in five to seven-year timeframes. When somebody says to me, congratulates Amazon on good quarter, which is a very common thing to say. You meet somebody, they're being nice, they looked at your financial results for the quarter it was a good quarter, I say thank you. But what I'm thinking to myself is that quarter, those quarterly results are actually pretty much fully baked about three years ago.

Like today, I'm working on a quarter that is going to happen in 2020, not next quarter. Next quarter, for all practical purposes is done already and it's probably been done for a couple of years. If you start to think that way, it changes how you spend your time, how you plan, where you put your energy, and your ability to look around corners gets better. So many things improve if you can take a long-term. By the way, it's not natural for humans, so it's a discipline that you have to build. The kind of get rich slowly schemes are not big sellers on infomercials. That's something that you have to sort of steel yourself for discipline and teach over time. So that what is Amazon, I would say really, it's a collection of principles and it's an approach that we deploy. It's fine, I dance into work.

Michael Beckerman: Me too. I'm not a good dancer. Get Rich slowly as a book, I probably should have gotten instead of this screenplay book.

Jeff Bezos: By the way, you know one of our award recipients earlier mentioned that you were happy you got rid of your banks. Me too. I hated my banks.

Michael Beckerman: So clearly, you do not take the success of Amazon lightly. You're very involved in the company. One of the great things about the internet many of your competitors are in this room tonight and competition is a click away. They're probably people in garages across the country trying to start a next great internet company like you did.

Jeff Bezos: For sure.

Michael Beckerman: What does keep you up at night when you think about the continued success of Amazon?

Jeff Bezos: Well, first of all, I'm gifted with sleeping really well. So the particular metaphor doesn't work for me, but I know what you mean, which is what could go wrong and what are you worried about. For me, the thing I worry about the most is that we would lose our way in one of those things. That we would lose our obsessive focus on customers or would somehow become short term oriented or would start to become overly cautious. You know, kind of failure averse and therefore unable to invent and pioneer. You cannot invent and pioneer if you cannot accept failure. To invent, you need to experiment and if you know in advance that it's going to work, it is not an experiment. That's a very important thing, they're inseparable twins, failure and invention. You have to be willing to do that.

You know it's always embarrassing to fail, but you have to say, no, that's not how this works. If I said to you, you have a 10% chance with a particular decision, a 10% chance of a 100x return, you should take that bet every time. But you're still going to be wrong nine out of 10 times, and it's going to feel bad nine out of 10 times. With technology, the outcomes, the results can be very long tailed. The payoff can be very asymmetric, which is why you should do so much experimentation. Everybody knows that if you swing for the fences, you hit more home runs, but you also strike out more. But with baseball, that analogy doesn't go far enough, because with baseball, no matter how well you connect with the ball, you can only get four runs. The success is capped at four runs, but in business, every once in a while you step up to the plate, and you hit the ball so hard, you get 1000 runs. When you have that kind of asymmetric payoff, and one bat can get you 1000 runs, it encourages you to experiment more. It's the right business decision to experiment more. It's also better for your customers, customers like the successful experiments. By the way, this is a giant misconception in a lot of young entrepreneurs and experienced entrepreneurs, that they meet, one of the things that is very fashionable right now is to talk about how disruptive their business plan is going to be. But invention is not disruptive, only customer adoption is disruptive. At Amazon, we've invented a lot of things that customers did not care about at all, and believe me, they were not disruptive to anyone.

So it's only when customers like the new way that anything becomes disruptive. Really it's just saying that if somebody comes to you with a business plan that they claim is disruptive, you should ask them to explain it to you in simpler language. The simpler language is why are customers going to adopt this? Why are they going to like it? Why is it better than the traditional way?

Michael Beckerman: So along those lines, we have some press and media in the room. Is there something that you think people get wrong about Amazon that surprises you when you read about it or see it in media coverage?

Jeff Bezos: Well, I don't know about wrong. First of all, we've been over 20 years on balance treated very fairly, by the media. Not every story that's ever been written about us is the way we would have written it if we were writing it ourselves. But on balance, very fairly treated. So, wrong might be too strong, I think there's a piece of our business, which is probably not fully appreciated the scale of it and what's happening and the energy and the dynamics around it. Which is the third-party seller part of our business. So, we have today roughly half of the company really is third-party sales, it's small businesses. There are 100,000 businesses on Amazon, where the businesses make $100,000 or more a year. It's turned into a gigantic service for them, we've even let them stow their products in our fulfillment centers, so that their products become prime eligible, which increases their sales.

A lot of people make their living on that way, and we've sort of extended that into other areas too. We have a platform called Kindle Direct Publishing, so authors can write books and then publish them directly. That's become very successful. So there are a lot of authors.

Michael Beckerman: Actually one of the employees has done that. Chris Hooton, our economist has a book published on that. It's very good.

Jeff Bezos: People make their living. I mean there are people who, I have so many emails from authors saying because of this program, I've been able to quit my job. They already have like 25 rejection letters from traditional publishers. Because their book didn't fit in a category or didn't seem right and so on, but readers disagreed. One of the things that you get when you let people, I think this is more like gardening. You kind of get all the nutrients right in the soil, and then you see what comes up. That's what happens with these third party businesses, we don't plan which books people are going to write. We just provide a service that makes it really easy for them to contact and reach readers and then they create these new things.

Same thing with Amazon Web Services, we created a set of tools and then software developers and companies that employ software developers, they figure out surprising and amazing things to build with these tools. Empowering these third parties to do things is probably starting with our third-party sellers and authors and AWS. Probably the biggest thing that most I would say consumers probably don't appreciate about Amazon. Good investors understand it very well.

Michael Beckerman

Love that. Okay, so 10 years ago, you mentioned AWS. So Amazon has changed so much in 10 years: 10 years ago, you barely in cloud computing.

Jeff Bezos: Yes.

Michael Beckerman: Certainly not.

Jeff Bezos: We've just started in cloud computing.

Michael Beckerman: Just started it and you're certainly not.

Jeff Bezos: Another overnight success. I've noticed all overnight successes take about 10 years.

Michael Beckerman: That's the right amount of time, probably. So we're five years away.

Jeff Bezos: Start something and just start the clock.

Michael Beckerman: Any year now. So Amazon's changed so much over that period of time, can you preview or predict maybe what Amazon is going to look like 10 years from now?

Jeff Bezos: Well, that's a very good question. I think on the outside, kind of the observable Amazon could change quite a bit. Just as you said there, 10 years ago, you wouldn't think that AWS would be such a significant contributor to the business and there could be more things like that in kind of 10-year timeframe that we don't know about. The one thing I hope will not change, of course, is that approach that I outlined at the beginning, the customer obsession, and the willingness to invent, patience, letting things develop, accepting failure as a path to getting success. By the way, one thing I should point out about failure, and this is a fine point, internally we take it, we know it and we don't need to talk about it much.

But there's a different kind of failure, which is not what you want. That's where you have operating history, and you do know what you're doing, and you just screw it up. So that's not a good failure, that's not an experiment, that's just bad operational excellence. Like if we've opened 130 fulfillment centers, we're on generation eight of our fulfillment center technology. If we open a new fulfillment center and just woof it, we have to do some internal examination, that's not an experiment, that's just bad execution. So there are different kinds of failure, and you need to make sure you're making the right kind of failure. The right kind of failure should be an invention, it's an experiment. You don't know if it's going to work and you know upfront that you don't know if it's going to work, that shouldn't be opening a new fulfillment center for us. Not sure I answered your question, I got distracted by failure. I've lived so comfortably with failure for so long that I revert there on a dime.

Michael Beckerman: It's an important distinction, though, between the two.

Jeff Bezos: It is, but the things that will stay the same over 10 years, hopefully the approach will stay the same. Then the other thing I would advise any entrepreneur, or large business or large organization, like a government organization, is you need to identify your big ideas. There are only two or three of them. The senior leader, the main job of a senior leader is to identify two or three important ideas, and then to enforce great execution against those big ideas. The good news is that the big ideas are usually incredibly easy to identify, you shouldn't need to think about them very much, you already know what they are, let me give you an example. For Amazon, the consumer business, the three big ideas are low prices, fast delivery, and vast selection. The way you know that they're the big ideas is because they're so obvious. The big ideas should be obvious and by the way, it's very hard to maintain a firm grasp of the obvious at all times. So little things can distract you from the obvious, but you have to back up and say these are the three big ideas. How do we always deliver things a little faster? How do we always reduce our cost structure so that we can have prices that are a little lower? The good thing about these big ideas is they will be stable in time. So I know for a fact that 10 years from now, customers are still going to like low prices.

No matter what happens with technology and everything else. No matter what happens people are going to like faster delivery. It is important for me to imagine a scenario where 10 years from now, a customer comes to me and says, Jeff, I love Amazon, I just wish you delivered a little more slowly. This is so inconceivable that you can have great conviction as a leader to continue to put energy into driving speed of delivery. In AWS, I know that customers, like low prices, they like availability, they don't want the services to be down, they like data security, it's not very hard to figure out what the big ideas are. Then you can keep putting energy into those things, you spin up those fire wheels, and they'll still be paying you dividends, 10 years from now. What I'm saying putting it in kind of a business context, but for those of you who are in government, these principles would apply identically to government organization. You should figure out what the big ideas are, and just spin up flywheels, get those things rolling, make sure that you've picked things that will still be true 10 years from now, 20 years from now.

Michael Beckerman: So on big ideas, artificial intelligence is something that I think has captured the imagination of Washington and probably the rest of the country and the world. What is Amazon's approach to artificial intelligence?

Jeff Bezos: Well first of all, artificial intelligence, machine learning, it is a Renaissance, it is a golden age. We are now solving problems with machine learning and artificial intelligence that were kind of in the realm of science fiction for the last several decades. Natural language understanding, machine vision problems, it really is an amazing Renaissance. For decades, AI researchers kind of struggled and made very, very slow progress. Over the last 10 years it looks like one of those s curves, you're just making a lot of progress very rapidly over the last 10 years. Machine learning and AI is a horizontal enabling layer, it will empower and improve every business, every government organization, every philanthropy. Basically, there's no institution in the world that cannot be improved with machine learning.

At Amazon, some of the things we're doing are super obvious. So they're kind of superficially obvious, and they're interesting, and they're cool. You should pay attention to this, I'm thinking about things like Alexa and Echo, our voice assistant, we're thinking about our autonomous Prime Air delivery drones, those things use a tremendous amount of machine learning, machine vision systems, natural language understanding, and a bunch of other techniques. Those are kind of the showy ones. I would say a lot of the value that we're getting from machine learning is actually happening kind of beneath the surface. It is things like improved search results, improved product recommendations for customers, improved forecasting, for inventory management, and literally hundreds of other things beneath the surface.

Then I'd say the most exciting thing that I think we're working on in machine learning is that we are determined, through

Amazon Web Services, where you have all these customers who are corporations and software developers, to make these advanced techniques accessible to every organization. Even if they don't have kind of the current class of expertise that's required right now, deploying these techniques for your particular institution's problems is difficult. It takes a lot of expertise and so you have to go compete for the very best PhDs in machine learning and get them in. It's difficult for a lot of organizations to win those competitions. We're in a great position because of the success of Amazon Web Services, to be able to put energy into making those techniques easy and accessible. We're determined to do that, I think we can build a great business doing that for ourselves. It would be incredibly enabling for organizations that want to use these sophisticated technologies to improve their own organizations.

Michael Beckerman: We have quite a few policymakers and elected officials and people from the administration here. I'd be remiss not to ask, how do you interface with the administration and how are you working with elected officials in general?

Jeff Bezos: Well, I think probably in the pretty normal ways, we have a fantastic public policy organization here. You guys already met Brian, Jay Carney. We have a bunch of people here in Washington, over time we've grown that group. We also do things at the state level, we're doing a little bit at certain municipal levels too. We work hard at it, it's really important to work hard at it, you can't just pretend that people know everything, and you don't have to educate them. We try to stay, I would say the main thing we tried to do, and I think we're pretty good at it, is stay very issues focused. We try to stay, you know, on the things that are specific to Amazon and our customers and our employees. As a company, our employees are free to have opinions about every issue they choose to have an opinion about. They can have opinions about anything they want. I feel like Amazon needs to be a little more laser focused than that on things that are important to our customers or to our employees as a group. I think our team does that, they keep us very disciplined in that way.

Michael Beckerman: I agree. I think you have a great team and just between us.

Jeff Bezos: Thank you. Yes, we'll cover your ears right.

Michael Beckerman: I have a few more questions. I know we're running out of time. You'd mentioned at a shareholders' meeting maybe last year, the previous year, about how Amazon's going to use it scale for sustainability.

Jeff Bezos : Yes.

Michael Beckerman: And environmentally, do you have anything you want to preview or update on?

Jeff Bezos: So you know for us, we have done a couple of things that I think everybody inside the organization is very proud of and it's been hard work, but it's paying off. We have a program called Frustration Free Packaging. We're working on it for roughly 10 years. It's a simple idea, but in credibly hard to execute. We go to manufacturers, and we say look, you are producing this thing in a four color printed package with a cellophane window and lots of twisty wire ties. Or worst case, what do they call those things? The clamshell packaging, where they seal it in indestructible plastic. You know I actually looked it up there is a Wikipedia entry for packaging rage or something like that there's a term for this. That Wikipedia entry has the number I don't remember the number now, but it's 1000s. The number of people who go to the emergency room per year trying to open that indestructible bubble packaging. Why do manufacturers put things in that kind of packaging?

It's not cheap, that packaging is expensive, it's hard to recycle. It has a bunch of flaws, but it shows off the product well. When it's hanging on a hook in a store shelf, as you walk by, you can actually see the product because it's sealed and clear plastic. Of course at Amazon that doesn't matter at all, we're going to show you great pictures of the product and videos of the product and customer reviews of the product. The product can be sealed in a tiny little cardboard box that's easy to open. We started this program, and we teach people how to make internet packaging, that is very efficient, easy to recycle, easy to open. Just in the past year, we have saved 55,000 tons of waste as a result of this program. We have now started putting solar cells on the roofs of all of our fulfillment centers, we're doing 15 this year. These are big fulfillment centers, they're about a million square feet each. We're covering them with solar cells, that'll cover about 80% of the fulfillment center's energy budget on an annual basis.

We are the largest purchaser in the world of renewable energy. I don't know, I'll screw up the figure because they garnered something like 3.6 million megawatt hours per year. We built solar farms and solar wind farms, we keep just rolling this out and we have a goal long term of being completely renewable. It'll take a long time, but the good news is these are not only great for the environment, they're good business decisions too. The technologies have improved to build a solar farm or a wind farm now. These are competitive technologies with natural gas powered plants and other things. You can actually do it and it feels like you're making a sensible business decision. I think a lot of companies will do this in the future, I think they should do it. We're having fun with all that.

Michael Beckerman: I have one final question that I have to ask you as we're running out of time, it's a shared passion of ours. I went to Space Camp as a child, and you have a rocket company.

Jeff Bezos: I knew I liked you right away.

Michael Beckerman: Yes, we have so much in common.

Jeff Bezos: Anybody that goes to Space Camp is my kind of person.

Michael Beckerman: Your rocket company, Blue Origin. It's really taking off, doing well. How do you see that company evolving in the future of space? What would you like to share on Blue Origin?

Jeff Bezos: First of all, I love space. I have been a space lover since I was a five-year-old boy. I feel like I won the lottery with Amazon, I know I won the lottery and now I'm investing those lottery winnings in Blue Origin, which is the space company. We are flying a suborbital tourism vehicle and we'll start taking people up hopefully in 2018. That's coming right up, working on it for more than 10 years. Hopefully, this overnight, success is taking longer than 10 years. I don't know, we'll see. We're also building an orbital vehicle called New Glenn, New Shepard is named for Alan Shepard, the first American in space, he went on a suborbital journey. New Glenn is named after the American hero, John Glenn, who was the first American to orbit the Earth. These are reusable boosters, fully reusable, that's the key to lowering the cost.

Our vision of Blue Origin is that we want millions of people living and working in space. My personal hope is that I live long enough to see this kind of dynamism in space, I want to see a whole economy, entrepreneurs in space, that I got to witness for the last 20 years on the internet. You know the problem with being an entrepreneur in the space arena is that the price of admission is so darn high. To do interesting things in space, kind of the beginning entry level is a few 100 million dollars. You're not going to get two kids in their dorm room doing something amazing in space. Whereas that's literally what happened to Facebook. On the internet, because the price of admission is so low, you can get these amazing experiments where like one kid in a dorm room does something and it turns into Facebook.

For Amazon's case, I started this thing with an incredibly small amount of capital. It was able to grow because we didn't need a lot to begin with. The heavy lifting was in place for Amazon, so I didn't need to build a transportation network, it existed already it was UPS and the Royal Mail and the US Postal Service and Deutsche Post and so on. I didn't have to build a telecommunications backbone to connect with my customers, it was there, it was called the internet and in fact, the internet was resting on top of the long-distance phone network at that time. You guys remember the dial up modem, some of you do. Some of you are too young to remember, some of you should go to a museum and see a dial up modem.

I recently showed a group of youngsters a payphone. I came across one and I was like, My God, guys come over here. This may be the last one, you have to see it. The point is that we didn't have to build a payment system, it already existed, it was called the credit card. Computers were already on every desk thanks to Microsoft, IBM, and Apple, and the more they being used for is to play games, not to buy things on Amazon. All that heavy lifting was in place. I would have such a good feeling, if I could be an 80-year-old guy and laying there thinking about my life. If I could say, look, there is now a bunch of entrepreneurs in space, because I took my Amazon lottery winnings and built the heavy lifting infrastructure that does take billions of dollars in capex, to lower the cost of access to space.

That's how you get millions of people living and working. By the way, we need that, for those of you who like to think about the future at all, you can do a simple calculation. We can argue about what limited resources on earth and so on and so on. But here's the calculation that you cannot argue with, which is you take current baseline energy usage on earth, compound it just a few percent a year for just a few 100 years, and you have to cover the entire surface of the earth in solar cells. We're going to have to decide, do we want a society of pioneering invention, expansion, growth? Or do we want a society of stasis? Personally, I believe because the earth is finite, if you want a society of stasis, first of all, I don't personally believe that stasis is even compatible with freedom. I think for me, that's a big problem.

Second of all, it's going to be dull. Stasis is going to be very dull, you don't want to live in the stasis world. Of course, we're going to continue to be more efficient too, we have been for hundreds of years, we've been getting more productive, more efficient, that trend is going to continue. But even so, we're going to want to use more energy, more energy per capita. I don't want to stabilize population, I would love for there to be trillion humans in the solar system. With a trillion humans, we would have 1000 Einsteins and 1000 Mozart's, it'd be an incredible symbol. Don't you want that dynamism? It'd be so much interesting. This is for your great, great, great-grandchildren, but what kind of world do you want them to live in? I want them to live in that expansive world that is learning more about the universe and moving out throughout the solar system. We have to do it.

Anyway, it's fun to work on that and I won so many lotteries in my life. I have the best parents in the world. My mom, Jackie and my dad, Mike. My mom had me when she was 17 in Albuquerque, New Mexico. She was still in high school, it was not cool, and she did an amazing job. My dad Mike is a Cuban immigrant who came here when he was 16 without his parents, did an amazing job. So those are the things that are your little gifts in life, my greatest admiration, by the way is withheld for those people, and I know several of them, who had terrible parents and still somehow made it through, that's hard. I had the opposite. I got lucky.

Michael Beckerman: Thank you, Jeff. Let's have a round of applause for Jeff Bezos.

Bezos Center of Innovation

Inauguration interview
(2013)

Hanson Hosein: When Jeff Bezos left New York City in 1994 to go west, young man, he hadn't decided if he would settle in Seattle or Portland. Along the way, he wrote the business plan for Amazon.com. And the rest is as much Internet history as it is Seattle's latest global success story. Now Bezos seeks to inspire the next generation of visionaries here at the Museum of History and Industry MOHIE. It's an ideal location right here on Lake Union. Bill Boeing pioneered commercial aircraft at the turn of the 20th century. Bill Gates launched a software empire less than 20 miles away and a few hundred yards from here where I stand, Bezos continues to grow Amazon even as he invests in space travel, journalism and social technologies, which is why we kick off our special series of the innovators with an exclusive interview with a man who lives by the motto; step by step ferociously, Jeff Bezos.
Jeff Bezos, welcome. Thank you. You are a man who embodies innovation. So what place is innovation actually have in a museum that wants to archive it? I mean, how do you inspire the kind of innovation you'd like to see in the world?

Jeff Bezos: Well, I think one of the things that you want is for kids when they come to a museum like this to be inspired by what's come before and to see what's possible and to see how individuals and companies invent pieces of the future and what that really means for our lives. And in Seattle, this is such a hotbed of innovation. It's really kind of remarkable, you know, on a per capita basis, I don't know of any place that has spawned more invention, more companies that really made a dent in the world.

Hanson Hosein: Yeah. And that geographic location right here in Seattle, right South Lake Union, close to Amazon. Why was it so important for you to actually put this monument to innovation or this inspiration to innovation right here?

Jeff Bezos: Well, the MOHAIE had already selected this location. They you know, they were moving for other reasons. And I just think Mohaie is the perfect environment for a center for innovation. That's kind of what they've been focused on from their founding.

Hanson Hosein: And when you think about our location, where Bill Boeing actually launched his first plane, you know, and we're 20 miles away from Bill Gates and now Jeff Bezos, this is probably it feels like the right place, like Seattle does have this incredible story around innovation.

Jeff Bezos: Yeah, there's something in the water here.

Hanson Hosein: I love that legend. I don't know if it's a legend or not, but you were in the car with your wife driving across the United States and you were doing the business plan as you were going there. Could you almost feel the pull of Go West, young man?

Jeff Bezos: Absolutely. In fact, you know, I had not made the final decision by the time the movers came and collected our stuff to take it from New York City to Seattle. I was still deciding between Seattle and Portland. And so I just told them we'll just get started heading west. And I'll let you know in a few days whether you should go to Seattle or Portland.

Hanson Hosein: What was the deciding factor?

Jeff Bezos: Well, the deciding factor was that Seattle is a little bit bigger. I looked at the number of flights per week and the airport and at that time I think it was three thousand flights a week coming out of Seattle and a thousand flights a week coming out of Portland. And so there are just a lot of little things that in a bigger city are a tiny bit easier.

Hanson Hosein: You mentioned that you wanted innovation to inspire this next generation. Why is it important to you? Why is it so important to you personally to make that happen?

Jeff Bezos: Well, I think, you know, I was very lucky kid. I was inspired by invention and self-reliance from a number of different people and from even watching the Apollo program as a little boy. And I think when little kids get inspired, you never know what might happen. It's a big deal and everything about our society gets better over time. I really do believe that I'm an optimist. You know, the myth of the good old days is usually just that, a myth. We have better medicine than we've ever had before. Everything, all of that is invention, it's people figuring out antibiotics, it's people figuring out new kinds of bio medicines, biotechnology. It's things that have been figured out with the kind of communication that we have, the freedom of speech we have now with the Internet. There are so many things that are getting better and a lot of that is powered by invention.

Hanson Hosein: Is there a particular methodology to that? Because I think that's really important, especially for young people to actually do that self-assessment and find that passion. Do you have any advice?

Jeff Bezos: I think that many, many kids and many grown-ups do figure out over time what their passions are. I think what happens, though, sometimes is that we let our intellectual selves overrule those passions. And so that's what needs to be guarded against. Kids are very good about knowing what their passions are.

Hanson Hosein: I love that because I think I've seen you described this way that you've always maintained that sense of wonder. I think that's what kids have. But we lose it somehow along the way.

Jeff Bezos: Yes, everybody, it's a gift. If you can keep your childlike sense of wonder and it helps with creativity, it helps to have fun. You know, you laugh more and play more if you keep that childlike sense of wonder.

Hanson Hosein: So, Bill Boeing, Bill Gates, Jeff Bezos, if you looked at what you brought and the legacy of innovation, how would you describe that?

Jeff Bezos: Well, I think what I would hope Amazon's legacy would be is Earth's most customer-centric company. What we have always wanted to do is raise the standard for what it means to be customer centric to such a degree that other organizations, whether they be other companies or whether they be hospitals or government agencies, whatever the organization is, they should look at Amazon as a role model and say, how can we be as customer centric as Amazon?

Hanson Hosein: Even competitors, I imagine. Right.

Jeff Bezos: Hopefully competitors as well. But if we could make you know, if that could be our legacy, that we kind of raised the general idea of what it means to be customer centric, that would be a huge accomplishment. It would be accomplishing a mission that's much bigger than ourselves.

Hanson Hosein: Harvard Business Review called you recently the most successful living CEO, Steve Jobs, obviously was listed as well. What does that mean to you as you consider your own leadership style?

Jeff Bezos: Well, I think if you look at the big ideas at Amazon, what we're really focused on is thinking long term, putting the customer at the center of our universe and inventing. Those are the three big ideas and they work well together. It's I don't think that you can invent on behalf of customers unless you're willing to think long term because a lot of inventions don't work. If you're going to invent, it means you're going to experiment. And if you're going to experiment, it means you're going to fail. And if you're going to fail, you have to think long-term. So these three ideas, customer centricity, long-term thinking and a passion for invention, those go together in our kind of Amazon cocktail. That's how we do it. And by the way, we have a lot of fun doing it that way.

Hanson Hosein: That long-term thinking especially, is what I find so powerful, because you have been known to be somebody who is going to plant seeds and just wait, how do you deal with the pressure of, say, Wall Street or if you have a dot-com crash? I've never seen you panic. You stay the course and you sort of stick to your script. How do you do that? And how do you advise us to sort of internalize that as well as a strategy?

Jeff Bezos: Well, I think that if you're straightforward and clear about the way that you're going to operate, then you can operate in whatever way you choose. And we don't even take a position on whether our way is the right way. We just claim it's our way. But, you know, Warren Buffett has a great saying along these lines. He says, you can hold a ballet and that can be successful and you can hold a rock concert and that can be successful. Just don't hold a ballet and advertise it as a rock concert. And so you need to be clear with all of your stakeholders, are you holding a ballet or you're holding a rock concert? And then people get to self-select in. You know, we hire people who are really motivated by building new customer experiences. They like to pioneer. They like the rate of change. They wake up in the shower motivated by thinking about customers. And occasionally somebody joins Amazon, who their primary motivation comes from thinking about competition or competitors. Those people can find Amazon a little dull, you know. So, again, it's not about right or wrong. It's just that different people are motivated by different things. And what happens with corporate cultures is that over time, people collect themselves in a way where they like that culture and then it becomes self-sustaining. We really have a group deep in our corporate DNA at this point, people who like to pioneer, people who like to invent. We like going down blind alleys, wandering in narrow alleys, wondering whether they're going to be blind alleys or whether they're going to open up into broad avenues. And that's fun for us.

Hanson Hosein: Well, that's really interesting because you're not guaranteeing success any time you go down those alleys, you don't know whether they're going to be blind. So when you look at success and you look at failure, how does it feel like when you're in the groove and you actually know you're on the path to success?

Jeff Bezos: Oh, it feels great. I mean, you know, it's you have to be in the mindset that you can accept blind alleys. But I'll tell you, the broad avenues are way more fun.

Hanson Hosein: Is there a particular recipe that you have in terms of how you actually innovate in that collaborative culture?

Jeff Bezos: I don't think there's a particular recipe, but there are elements of what we do that I think help. So one of them is that inside our culture, we understand that even though we have some big businesses, new businesses start out small. And so, you know, it would be very easy for, say, the person who runs are US books category to say, why are we doing these experiments with these things? I mean, that generated a tiny bit of revenue last year. Why don't we instead focus those resources and all that brainpower on this books category which is a big business for us and instead that would be a natural thing to have happened. But instead, inside Amazon, you know, when a new business reaches some small milestone of sales, email messages go around and everybody's giving virtual high fives for reaching that milestone. I think it's because we know from our past experiences that big things start small. You know, the biggest oak starts from an acorn. And you've got to recognize if you want to do anything new, you've got to be willing to let that acorn grow into a little sapling and then finally into a small tree. And maybe one day it'll be a big business on its own,

Hanson Hosein: In fact, that's one of the models of one of your initiatives, but Gradatim Ferociter, what does that mean to you?

Jeff Bezos: Well, it means step by step ferociously. And it's the motto for Blue Origin. And basically, you can't skip steps. You have to put one foot in front of the other. Things take time. There are no shortcuts, but you want to do those steps with passion and ferocity.

Hanson Hosein: Amazing about your successes is that your timing was good, too. How does an innovator actually identify that historical momentum, that Kittyhawk moment? You recognized what was happening with the Internet. And you said, you know what, there's actually a room for me to start with books and then move on. How do you do that? How do you find the time and the momentum of the zeitgeist?

Jeff Bezos: Well, I think to some degree you follow your passions and then wait. You know, you have to hope the wave catches you. I was always interested in computers. I was always interested in software. I was always a big reader. And so it made me alert to things like the Internet and the possibility that you could build a bookstore online that would have universal selection. And that was really the founding idea of Amazon. I think everybody has their own passion, their own thing that they're interested in. And then you're very alert to the things that are in the sphere of influence of that passion,

Hanson Hosein: So your passion has led you to change the world frankly, with Amazon, but yet you've got Blue Origin, you've got Bezos Explorations. Why can't somebody like you just rest on your laurels?

Jeff Bezos: Oh well, you know, I love what I do. I also have four kids. I have a wife that I love. I have a lot of passions and interests. At Amazon, the rate of change is so high. And I love that, I love the pace of change. I love the fact that I get to work with these smart, big smart teams. The people I work with are so smart and they all are self selected for loving to invent on behalf of customers. And so, you know, it's not doing I love every moment of every day? No. That's why they call it work. There are always things that I don't enjoy. But if I'm really objective about it and I look at it, I'm so lucky to be working alongside all these passionate people and I love it. Why would I go sit on a beach?

Hanson Hosein: I think that's important, authenticity and passion for anybody who's looking to innovate. The technology, the rate of change. I saw Vinton Cerf recently, he's considered to be one of the fathers of the Internet, say that we are now in the era of permissionless innovation, meaning that we don't necessarily need to wait for permission from an institution like a government or a corporation to do something. What does that mean to you in your position?

Jeff Bezos: Well, I think that's largely correct. I mean, in fact, some of the things that Amazon has the tools that we provide are designed to make it easy for people to do what Vince is calling permissionless invention, things like Amazon Web Services so that you don't have to build your own data center. You really can be a college student in a dorm room and you have access to unlimited compute facilities through Amazon Web Services, same thing with Kindle Direct Publishing and a platform for publishers, there are no gatekeepers, it's self-service. You know, if you've gotten thirty-seven rejection letters, try it yourself.

Hanson Hosein: That's right. Thanks to you.

Jeff Bezos: You know, and then there are other things where I think the scale is such that you do need big capital. I mentioned earlier, you're not going to build a brand new carbon fiber plane like the 787 without the resources of a Boeing. So you know that you're not going to do in your dorm room. You're not going to invent Kindle in your dorm room either to build a consumer electronics device like Kindle and to pull all the books together for it and so on, that's a big team effort. Many hundreds of people working over a number of years. So some things are still require big teams, lots of resources, many years to pull together. And those are very important innovations, too. But he's right that we're on a trend line where more every passing year, more powerful things can be done by small teams.

Hanson Hosein: And that's interesting because scale and size matter. But the danger is if somebody successful as you or as Amazon being successful, you have a lumbering, potentially a lumbering giant. How do you remain nimble? Because there is somebody in their dorm room who could eat you up for lunch the next day? You know,

Jeff Bezos: My belief on this is, first of all, that's completely correct. You can never assure anybody that that can't happen. But I think if you have a customer-centric culture, that cures a lot of ills. Let's say you're the leader in a particular arena, if you're competitor focused and you're already the leader, then where does your energy come from? Whereas if you're customer focused and you're already the leader, customers are never satisfied. So if you're customer focused, you're always waking up wondering, how can we make that customer say wow. Our energy, our passion, we want to impress our customers. We want them to say, wow.

Hanson Hosein: And that accountability really matters to you as well.

Jeff Bezos: We love it. It's that kind of divine discontent that comes from observing customers and noticing that things can always be better.

Hanson Hosein: When you look at education. Amazon has this incredible technology. Is there ways to sort of turn Amazon's technology towards helping the educational challenges that we face in this country right now?

Jeff Bezos: Yeah, I think there are. And in fact, we're doing some things with Kindle now. We have something called Whisper Cast, which lets schools manage fleets of Kindles. But I think that's just the tip of the iceberg. I think that if you look at things like the Khan Academy and some of the other things out there on the horizon, I think there is a real chance that technology may ultimately fulfill its promise of helping with education. I think people have hoped for that for a long time, and it hasn't really ever come to fruition, not in a big way. But I'm still very optimistic that that may happen. And in fact, maybe some of the kids who visit Mohai will be the ones who will really figure it out.

Forum on Leadership at the the Bush Center

A Conversation with Kenneth Hersh, President and CEO of the Bush Center.

Kenneth Hersh: Well, Jeff, welcome to Dallas. I'm excited that you can see what a city that really wants you here looks like right guys?

Sorry, that was too tempting. So I've left 30 seconds here, just in case there's a little real estate deal that you want to. It's very nice to be here. Alright, I tried. I tried the before we get started, I do want to I do want to thank the sponsors tonight Amarillo National Bank, and Highland Capital Management. This is a multi faceted event. We're here with SMU, our great partner. We're here as the engage event sponsored by Highland capital. And we're also here is the culminating conversation of our forum on leadership. And this has been a great couple of days with mano Priscilla Chan, Governor Hickenlooper Martinez, Ben Bernanke, and Hank Paulson, many others, and Condi Rice and President Mrs. Bush talking about leadership. So I want to talk about leadership. Yeah. And the, the first thing to really talk about is to I want to take you back to, to the beginning. And in 1995, you started Yep. You went public in 97. And all adjust for stock splits. But you raised stock, right, you issued shares at $1.50 a share. That's right, in 1988, your revenue was $600 million, and your last 125 million, but your stock had gone to $55 a share. So you doubled down, sales went up threefold, you lost another 400 million, but your stock went up to $76 $27 billion of market cap, your personal net worth of 9 billion. Take us back to that time where the market is telling you you're doing great. But you have red ink in the company, you took on $2 billion of debt from 99 201. While you tripled why you doubled sales yet again? What were you thinking back then?

Jeff Bezos: Well, that's a great, great question. And it is kind of fun to go back and think about those days. You know, in those days when we had I don't know, when I started the company, and it was just one person. And then there were 10 people, and today they're almost 600,000 people. So there's a lot of change. But back in that time, we were still pretty small company, by most standards, but we were growing fast. And it was very exciting. You know before, I was driving all the packages to the post office myself. I knew the UPS guy so well, that he would let me in even like five minutes after closing. So it was I hoped one day we'd be able to afford a forklift. It was that kind of operation. We were so inefficient with our operations and logistics in those early days when there were just 10 of us that I didn't have packing tables, we were packing on the floor, on our hands and knees. And I said to one of the software engineers who was packing alongside me, you know, what we should do, we should get kneepads. And he looked at me, like I was the dumbest guy he'd ever seen in his life. And he said, Jeff, we should get packing tables. The next day, I got packing tables, and it doubled our productivity. But by the era you're talking about, we had gone public, and you're writing on a split adjusted basis, it's $1.50 a share in today's terms. The market became very quickly kind of an internet bubble market and the stock prices went up very very high. When I raised the initial funding for Amazon, I had to talk to 60 prospective investors to raise a million dollars and I raised a million dollars from 22 different investors $50,000 at a time, and they got 20% of the company for a million dollars. That was in 95. But just two or three years later, you know Stanford MBA with no business experience could raise $25 million with a single phone call if they had an internet business plan.

So the whole thing in just two or three years, the excitement, really, as we could certainly see, when the bubble burst in the year 2000, the hyperbolic excitement about the internet had infected everybody. I liked our business and I liked the fundamentals of our business, but also knew that the stock price was disconnected from what we're doing on a day to day basis. I was always preaching, we would have all hands meetings, and there was a small number of employees at that time, in 97 I think we would have had 100 employees, we would have all hands meetings and I would say, look, remember the great quote from Benjamin Graham, that in the short run, the stock market is a voting machine, in the long run, it's a weighing machine. So don't think about the daily stock prices going up, every day the stock price is going up. And I didn't want because all the employees had stock options, and I didn't want them counting their success that way. So would say, look, when the stock is up 30% in a month, don't feel 30% smarter, because when it's down 30% in a month, then you're going to have to feel 30% dumber and it's not going to feel as good, right? And it was good that I kind of laid that groundwork because you know, sure enough, in the year 2000, the whole thing came tumbling down. I think Amazon went back at $6, I don't even know if that's on a split adjusted basis. I think that probably that was below a split adjusted basis, probably below $1.

Kenneth Hersh: Did you ever doubt the business model at that point?

Jeff Bezos: No, it's very interesting to me, because I had all the internal metrics on, you know, how many customers we had was growing. I could see, people thought we were losing money, because we were selling dollar bills for 90 cents. Even though we were very clear that we were not, we had high fixed costs, and we had positive contribution margin. I just knew that it was a fixed cost business. As soon as we reached a sufficient scale, we would have a very good business. That was the understanding of the fixed nature of our expenses relative to physical world retail is what led us to have the get big fast strategy. We knew that our economics would be very much improved if we could have a sufficient scale. So we worked hard.

Kenneth Hersh: So at that time, you're preaching the benefits of e-commerce and really disintermediating the business. So fast forward to today. Now we have content. We have physical Amazon stores, we have Amazon cashierless stores, which we used to call shoplifting. That's right. And then buying Whole Foods here for a Texas company. How does that fit together in your vision? And then how do you manage these disparate businesses with with different cost structures now?

Jeff Bezos: By the way, maybe just finishing up a little on that prior point before I answer that question. Also with the memory of Barbara Bush, in all of our minds. I think a lot of people in this room are entrepreneurs, started their own businesses, done various things, taking risks of various kinds. And I think the one of the precursors, one of the foundational thing, to being able to take risk is to have had some kind of support from somebody, to have some mentors, somebody who loves you, these are the kinds of things that build up and allow you to jump off into uncharted terrain, and do something new because you know you have a support system of one kind or another. And I certainly did so. For me, I just want to point out that I feel very strongly that I've won a lot of lotteries. Amazon is one of the lotteries that I've won, but I had a big lottery with my parents. My dad is a Cuban immigrant. He came here when he was 16 years old and speaking English, he is a great guy, and my mother had me when she was 17 years old. So she was a pregnant at 16 year old in Albuquerque, New Mexico in high school, which was not cool. And she made it work and her parents, my grandparents helped her with that whole thing and made that all work. And if you don't get that kind of support somehow it doesn't have to be your parents. Sometimes you get lucky it's a grandparent or it's a friend or a family friend or a teacher. It can be somebody but you need that somebody to step into your life. And that's a lottery that I suspect a lot of people in this room have also won just like me. So the question go Amazon go and all this, we do so many different things. So this is a question I sometimes get, how can you do so many different things? Why don't you stick to the knitting, the kind of traditional advice would be to stay focused and keep the business simple. The way I think about this is, we actually do stick to one thing, it's just not described, the business of web services, which is big enterprises buying compute services from us (AWS).

We have our retail business, we have Amazon Studios, which is making original content, Amazon Go, the things you listed. The cultural thread that runs through all these things is the same, we have a few principles at Amazon kind of core values that we go back to over and over again. If you look at each of the things we do, you would see those run straight through everything. So the first one, and by far the most important is customer obsession. We talk about it as customer obsession, as opposed to competitor obsession.

I have seen over and over again, companies say they are customer focused, but really, when I pay close attention to them, I believe they're competitor focused. That is just a completely different mentality. By the way, competitor, focus can work, but I don't think it works in the long run, as well as customer focus. For one thing, once you're the leader, if your whole culture is competitor obsessed, it's kind of hard to stay energized and motivated if you're out in front. Whereas customers are always unsatisfied, they're always discontent, they always want more. And so no matter how far, you get out there in front of your competitors, you're still behind your customers, they are always pulling you along. So customer obsession is a deep principle that underlies everything we do. An other one is eagerness to invent, we love to pioneer. And when we have done by the way, whenever we have tried to do something in a kind of me-too fashion, we have failed at it, we need to have something that is differentiated, unique, something that customers are going to like that we're leading with. So that's another element that works for us.

An other one is long term thinking we are willing to take some time and be patient with our business initiatives. And that runs through everything. So a lot of our competitors might have two to three year kind of timeframe, we might have more than five to seven years sort of timeframe. And then the last one is operational excellence. So literally, how do you have high standards around identifying defects, fixing defects at the root, all those kinds of things that lead to what I think also can be in a simpler way just stated as professionalism, want to do things right, just for the sake of doing them right.

Kenneth Hersh: Now that you have about 600,000 employees, I calculate it, you're adding about 250 people a day. You've mentioned that you're trying to fend off day two. And you said the day two is status, followed by irrelevance, followed by excruciatingly painful decline, followed by death, that's why it is always day one. How's does that work?

Jeff Bezos: Well, so day one, this is a phrase that we use at Amazon all the time. I've been using it since my first annual shareholder letter from 20 years ago. We say it's always day one, and it needs to be day one for the reason that you just mentioned. So the real question for me is, how do you go about maintaining a day one culture, you know, it's great to have the scale of Amazon, we have financial resources, we have lots of brilliant people, we can accomplish great things. We have global scope, we have operations all over the world. But the downside of that is that you can lose your nimbleness, you can lose your entrepreneurial spirit, you can lose that kind of heart that small companies often have. And so if you could have the best of both worlds, if you can have that entrepreneurial spirit and heart, while at the same time having all the advantages that come with scale and scope, think of the things that you could do. So the question is how do you achieve that? The scale is good because it makes you robust, you know, a big boxer can take a punch to the head. The question is you also want to dodge those punches, so you'd like to be nimble, you want to be big and nimble.

I find there a lot of things that are protective of the day one mentality, I already spent some time on one of them, which is customer obsession. I think that's the most important thing if you can, and it gets harder as you get bigger. When you're a little tiny company, 10 person startup company, every single person in the company is focused on the customer. When you get to be a bigger company, you've got all the middle managers, and you've got all these layers. And those people are not on the front lines, they're not interacting with customers every day. They're insulated from customers. And they start to manage not the customer happiness directly, but manage through proxies, like metrics and processes, and some of those things can become bureaucratic. So it's very challenging. But one of the things that happens is the decision making velocity slows down. I think the reason one why that happens is that people, all Junior executives inside the big company, start to model all decisions as if they are heavyweight, irreversible, highly consequential decisions. And so even two way doors, you could make a decision and if it's the wrong decision, you can just back up through the door and try again, even those reversible decisions start to be made with heavyweight processes. And so you can teach people that the're pitfalls and traps and then teach them to avoid those traps. This is what we're trying to do at Amazon, so that we can maintain our inventiveness, our hearts and our kind of small companies spirit, even if we have the scale and scope of a larger company.

Kenneth Hersh: So 600,000 people small company, that's a trick. At the bush center we focus on leadership. And I know that you're also a voracious reader. That you're fond of a book by Nassim Taleb called the Black Swan, it's about human tendencies to reduce things to anecdotal stories. And to shield us from sort of the randomness of the way things actually happen.

Jeff Bezos:
Bezos: We humans can create a narrative around anything, connect any sequence of facts and create a narrative?

Kenneth Hersh: So how do you infect that throughout the whole organization, when you have that many layers?

Jeff Bezos: Well, I think what I would say about that, it's really a little different from the way the Black Swan talks about anecdotes. But I'm actually a big fan of anecdotes in business, not building a narrative structure around them necessarily.
I still have an email address that customers can write to, I see most of those emails, I don't answer very many of them anymore, but I see them and I forward them, some of them, the ones that catch my curiosity, I forward them to the executives in charge of that area with a question mark. That question mark is just a shorthand for, can you look into this? Why is this happening? What's going on?
What I find very interesting is that we have tons of metrics. We have weekly business reviews with these metric decks. We

know so many things about our customers, whether we're delivering on time, whether the packages have too much air in them, or wasteful packaging, we have so many metrics that we monitor. The thing I have noticed is that when the anecdotes and the data disagree, the anecdotes are usually right, there's something wrong with the way you're measuring it. You need to run something on what you're doing. When you're shipping billions of packages a year for sure you need good data and metrics are you delivering on time? Do you deliver on time in every city? Are you delivering on time to apartment complexes? Are you delivering on time in certain countries? You do need the data. But then you need to check that data with your intuition and your instincts and you need to teach that to the all the senior executives and junior executives.

Kenneth Hersh: So if you're not answering your emails, can you give us your cell phone maybe a text? Do you still have the two pizza rule and no PowerPoints?

Jeff Bezos: Oh yes, the two pizza team, we try to create teams that are no larger than can be fed with two pizzas. We call that the two pizza team rule. No PowerPoints are used inside of Amazon. So every meeting we have when we hire a new executive from the outside, this is the weirdest meeting culture you will ever encounter, new executives have a little bit of culture shoc on their first Amazon meeting. What we do is that somebody has prepared for the meeting a six-page memo, a narratively structured memo that's got real sentences, topic sentences and verbs and not just bullet points. It lays out and suppose to create the context for what will then be a good discussion. We read those memos silently in the meeting, so it's like a study hall. Everybody sits around the table and we read silently for usually about half an hour, however long it takes us to read the document. And then we discuss it, it's so much better than the typical PowerPoint presentation for so many reasons.

Kenneth Hersh: One author said that that takes you back to River Oaks Elementary School in Houston, where you started, where they started with a reading with a silent reading exercise.

Jeff Bezos: I never made that connection. But, you never know where things come from. I did have a great experience there. So I definitely recommend the memo over the PowerPoint. And the reason we read them in the room, by the way, is because just like high school kids, executives will bluff their way through the meeting as if they've read the memo. Because we're busy, you've got to actually carve out the time for the memo to get read, and that's what the first half hour of the meeting is for. Then everybody's actually read the memo, they're not just pretending to have read it.

Kenneth Hersh: That's pretty effective. How has your leadership style changed Over the years?

Jeff Bezos: It's changed a lot, mostly just because it had to, the company has changed so much. In companies of 10 people or 100 people, I can be involved in every decision, not just the objectives, like what are we going to do, but even the methods, how are we going to do it.
And as the company gets bigger, you know, the CEO or the founder, or whoever is leading the company cannot be involved in all the decisions, they certainly cannot be involved in the methods of how things are going to get done. So you do have to change your leadership approach as the company scales. But the principles of the company have not changed.
In fact, I probably spend more of my time now on culture and trying to set high standards for things like customer obsession, inventiveness and things like that. For me, I'm kind of a teacher now, so It has changed quite a bit and I have this great luxury, I love my job, I tap dance into work. I just got back from an amazing vacation in Norway. I got to go dogsledding and to a wolf preserve, all this really cool stuff. But I couldn't wait to get back to work, because it's so fun, and the reason why it is so fun for me, is I get to work in the future.
In my job, I have very limited kind of day to day operational needs, I've constructed my job so that I don't have to be pulled into the present. I can stay two or three years in the future. And actually, I'm always advising my senior team, the people who report to me that they should organize themselves in the same way. We're big enough now that they need to be able to look around corners. if something pulls me into the present,

it's because something has gone wrong. It's a kind of a firefighting exercise. That's not how you should be running a business of this scale. So it's changed a lot.

Kenneth Hersh: Okay, so following up with that, you were quoted as saying, I believe you have to be willing to be misunderstood overall, to innovate. So how are you misunderstood?

Jeff Bezos: if you're going to do anything new or innovative, you have to be willing to be misunderstood. And if you can't tolerate that, then for God's sake, don't do anything new or innovative. Every important thing we've done has been misunderstood, often by well meaning sincere critics, sometimes of course by self interested, insincere critics.
I'll give you an example; 1000 years ago, we started this thing called customer reviews, and we let customers review books, we only sold books at that time. Customers could come in and rate a book between one to five stars, and they could write a text based review. You guys are very familiar with this, now it's a very normal thing. But back then, this was crazy. And the book publishers did not like this. Because of course, not all the reviews are positive. And the got a letter from one publisher that said, I have a good idea for you, why don't you just publish the positive customer reviews. I thought about this, and the argument he is making to me is that our sales would go up, if we just published the positive customer reviews. I thought, I don't actually believe that. Because I don't think we make

money when we sell something, we make money when we help someone make a purchase decision.
It is just a slightly different way of looking at it. Because the part of what people are paying us for, is helping them make a purchase decision. And if you think about it that way, then you want the negative reviews too. Of course, it has been extremely helpful for people to have negative customer reviews. And by the way, it's come full circle now, where the product manufacturers use the customer reviews to improve the next generation of the product. So it's actually helping the whole ecosystem.
Now nobody criticizes customer reviews. In fact, if in the year 2018, some ecommerce company were to say, we're only going to publish the positive customer reviews, that would be the crazy thing and would get criticized. So the new and innovative quickly becomes the new normal, it's then the new incumbent idea and doesn't get criticized, when, by the way more generally. What I preach at Amazon to all of our employees, is when we are criticized there is a simple process that you need to go through. First, you look at yourself in the mirror and decide is your critic right? Do you agree? Are we doing something wrong? If you are, change, and by the way, if you look yourself in the mirror, and you decide that your critic is wrong, as we did with the customer reviews, then do not change, no matter how much pressure is brought to bear, do the right thing. In that case as well, you have to have a deep keel.

Kenneth Hersh: Good. So why don't we shift to personal away from Amazon a little bit? If, if you could write your legacy? What would you want your legacy to read?

Jeff Bezos: world's oldest man? I stole that, that's not original. But I would love it, let's work on that. I keep telling my biotech friends hurry to hell guys, come on.

Probably if you think long term, and I can talk about this in great length. If you take a really long run view, many decades, maybe even couple hundred years? I think the most important work that I'm doing, and I get increasing conviction on this with every passing year, is the work I'm doing at Blue Origin on space travel.

Kenneth Hersh: Well, why don't we talk about that? I think from a vision standpoint, I think people should appreciate the horizon that you have. So let's talk about your kind of view. I'll call it your near term objectives, we'll say 75 years, and then your long term objectives 100 to 300 years from that.

Jeff Bezos: Well, first of all, you don't choose your passions, your passions choose you. All of us are gifted with certain passions, the people who are lucky are the ones who get to follow those things. I always advise our young employees, I meet with interns as well, and my kids too, you can have a job, you can have a career or you can have a calling. And if you can somehow figure out how to have a calling, you've hit the

jackpot, because that's the big deal. Most people don't ever get there, you're very lucky if you have a career, a lot of people just end up with a job.
For me, I have been interested in rockets, space travel, propulsion, since I was a five year old boy, and I have spent a tremendous amount of time thinking about it. So it's not like I really have a choice to follow this passion. It has captured me, but I think it's very important that we go out into space as a civilization. And the reason is not the one that I think is very common, many reasons there, are given. One of the reasons that is out there, and it's a very old idea. One of the people who first articulated very well is Arthur C. Clarke, he said: all civilizations become spacefaring or extinct. That even may be technically true in a long run, kind of long enough horizon.
The idea that kind of came to me is, we've got all our eggs in one basket, and we need a plan B. If we had a civilization elsewhere on another planet, somewhere in the solar system, then when Earth gets destroyed, humanity will still be fine. I find this particular argument incredibly unmotivated. We have now sent robotic probes to every planet in this solar system. Believe me, this is the best one. It is not close. To my friends who want to move to Mars, I have an idea for you. Why don't you first for a year, move to the top of Mount Everest, because the top of Mount Everest is a garden paradise compared to Mars.
This planet is a gym, this planet is unbelievable. And as you travel around, the more you travel around you, the more you see how incredible it is. And I'm not even just talking about

nature, I'm talking about the civilization we built in the urban cities that we have, and all these amazing things, so we need to protect it.
Now, I'm not even talking about protecting it from asteroids, or nuclear holocaust, although all these things are probably important and valid. We don't need to worry about that, because we have something more certain that is a problem. That is if you take current baseline energy usage on earth today, global energy usage, and compound that at just 3% a year, then in just a few hundred years, you're gonna have to cover the entire surface of the earth and solar cells. That's how powerful compounding is. So and by the way, we have been growing energy usage at a few percent a year for a long time. Our civilization has a lot of advantages, because we increase our energy usage, the human body, if we in our state of nature, if you are just an animal in the state of nature, your body, your metabolic rate, uses about 100 watts of power. But as a modern person living in a developed country, the civilizational per capita metabolic rate is 11,000 watts, we use a lot of energy. That's about as much energy as a blue whale uses. There are billions of us, and most of us aren't even living in the kind of lifestyle of a developed country yet, but they will be very soon, we hope they will be we want them to. So, you're going to face a choice, you won't face this choice, and I will not face this choice, but your grandchildren's grandchildren will face this choice. Do you want to live in a world of stasis?

Jeff Bezos: Or do you want to have a trillion humans living in the solar system? The solar system is big, Earth is small, we capture a tiny earth surface is so small, it captures a tiny, tiny fraction of the solar output. So once you got into space you have for practical purposes, once again, unlimited resources. And the solar system can easily support a trillion humans you got a trillion humans then you'd have 1000 Mozart's and 1000 Einsteins, and so on. That would be a dynamic, incredible civilization in which you would want your grandchildren's grandchildren to live in.

I think ultimately, Earth becomes zoned residential and light industrial, and we'll have universities here and beautiful parks and houses, but we won't have big factories here. All of that will be much better done in space where we have access to much higher quality resources. You know, that's a multi hundred year vision.

And my piece of this vision is I'm taking my Amazon lottery winnings, and I'm converting them into reusable rocket vehicles, so that we can lower the cost of access to space. Because right now the price of admission to do interesting things in space is just too high. If I look at what Amazon was able to do 20 years ago, we didn't have to build a transportation network, it already existed, that heavy lifting was in place, we didn't have to build a payment system, that heavy lifting had already been done, it was the credit card system, we didn't have to build a computer on every desk that had already been done, mostly for playing games by the way, and so on. So all the pieces of heavy lifting, were already in place 20 years ago. And that's why with a million dollars, I could start this company today. There are even better examples on the internet over the last 20 years, Facebook started in a dorm room, I guarantee you two kids cannot build a giant space company in their dorm room, it's impossible. But I want to create the heavy lifting infrastructure, kind of the hard part. So that the future generation, two kids in a dorm room will be able to create a giant space company. That's the goal. You're not gonna to achieve the vision that I just laid out of a trillion humans living in space and having this dynamic world without a big industry made up of 1000s of companies. But it has to start with making the vehicles much more productive. Right now, you use a rocket once and you throw it away. And that is just a very expensive way to do business.

It's just too high if I look at what Amazon was able to do 20 years ago, we didn't have to build a transportation network. It already existed. That heavy lifting was in place. We didn't have to build a payment system. That heavy lifting had already been done. It was the credit card system. We didn't have to build, put a computer at every desk that had already been done to mostly for playing games, by the way, and so on. So all the pieces of heavy lifting were already in place 20 years ago. And that's why, as with a million dollars, I could start this company today, you know, and then there are even better examples on the Internet over the last 20 years, you know, Facebook started in a dorm room. I guarantee you two kids cannot build a giant space company in their dorm room. It's impossible. But I want to create the heavy lifting infrastructure, kind of do the hard part so that a future, the future generation to kids in a dorm room will be able to create a giant space company. So that's the goal. And then because you. Thank you. You're not going to you're not going to achieve the vision that I just laid out of a trillion humans living in space and having this dynamic world without a big industry made up of thousands of companies. But it has to start with making the vehicles much more productive. And right now, you use a rocket once and you throw it away. And that is just a very expensive way to do business.

Kenneth Hersh: So can I talk then about another element with to get you to discuss your vision? This may not be germane to the work you're doing, but you are one of the great thinkers, artificial intelligence pros and cons. We've heard people talk about the great benefits. We've heard about disrupting and changing and leaving us all in a jobless society. We've heard autonomous weapons are a disaster. What is your vision of where in artificial intelligence is going to go? And also some of the more cautionary benefits?

Jeff Bezos: Well, you mentioned a few things and each of those is worth visiting, because they're different. I think autonomous weapons are extremely scary. By the way, do not need general A.I. So right now, the things that we know how to do, you should think of those things as what is called narrow A.I., things like machine vision and so on. To build incredibly scary autonomous weapons, you do not need general A.I. The techniques that we already know and understand are perfectly adequate. Some of these weapons are in fact very scary. I don't know what is the solution to that, but smart people need to be thinking about that. Doing a lot of R&D, you'd have to have a big treaty like the Geneva Convention or something that would help regulate these weapons, because they actually have a lot of issues. So that one, I think, is genuinely scary. The idea that there's going to be a general A.I. overlord that subjugates us or kills us all, I think is not something to worry about, I think that is overhyped. First of all, we're nowhere close to knowing how to build a general AI, something that could set its own objectives. It's not even a valid research area.

We're so far back on that one. So I think, that's a very long-term prospect that it could even happen. But second of all, I think it's unlikely that such a thing's first instincts would be to exterminate us. That would seem surprising to me. Much more likely, it will help us, because we know we're perfectly capable of hurting ourselves, maybe we could use some help. So I'm optimistic about that one, and I certainly don't think we need to worry about it today. And then the jobless, is AI going to put everybody out of work? I am not worried about this. I find that all of us, I include myself, we are so unimaginative about what future jobs are going to look like and what they're going to be. If I took you back in time, one hundred years when almost everyone was a farmer and I told you at some big farming convention, in the year 2018, there is going to be a job occupation called massage therapist. They would not have believed it. In fact, I was telling this story to a friend and he said, Jeff, forget massage therapist, there are dog psychiatrists.

Kenneth Hersh: You will probably find one on Amazon.

Jeff Bezos: I went and looked that up on the Internet. Sure enough, you can easily hire a psychiatrist for your dog. You know, we humans like to do things and we like to be productive. We will figure out things to do and we will use these tools to make ourselves more powerful. In fact, what I predict is that jobs will get more engaging, because a lot of the jobs today are quite routine, they are not necessarily anybody's, as I said before, career or calling. So, I predict that because of artificial intelligence and its ability to automate certain tasks, that in the past were impossible to automate, that not only will we have a much wealthier civilization, but that the quality of work will go up very significantly and that a higher fraction of people will have callings and careers, relative to today.

Kenneth Hersh: Can I bring you back down to the present a little bit? You bought the Washington Post a few years ago, is it going the way you thought it would go?

Jeff Bezos: Much better, much faster. The Post is profitable today. I bought the post in 2013, the Post was still a fantastic institution at that time, but it was in great financial difficulty.

It's a fixed cost business, most of all publishing is. Their revenues over about six years from 2007-2008 to 2013 had been cut in half, from a billion dollars a year to half a billion dollars a year. That in a fixed cost business puts a tremendous amount of pressure on the business. They needed to reduce the size of the newsroom, layoff reporters and it was very difficult. Don Graham, whose family had owned the paper for a long period of time, contacted me through an intermediary. Actually, we've known each other for almost 20 years, and I was very surprised. But he said that he was interested in selling the paper, I said, look, I'm not the right buyer, I don't know anything about the newspaper business. He said, we don't need any of that, we've got lots of people who understand newspaper business. We need somebody who understands the Internet better. This was a great act of love, because the paper had been in their family for a long time and he cared more about the paper than he cared about his ownership of it.

And if any one of you know him, he's an incredible gentleman, just a wonderful guy. After several conversations, he finally convinced me that I could help. Then I had to convince myself of a couple of things. One was, did I really believe it was an important institution? And that for me was a very quick gate to get through. I felt very powerfully that it was an important institution. I do believe that democracy dies in darkness. I think that the paper resides in Washington, DC, the capital city of the United States of America, the most powerful country in the world needs a paper like The Washington Post. And so it was easy to decide it's an important institution. I would not have bought and tried to help turn around a financially upside down, salty snack food company. You know, I just have better things to do. I might buy a really well run healthy salt food snack company that would just be an investment. The second gate I had to go through after that was I really wanted to convince myself that it wasn't hopeless because if it had been hopeless, I wouldn't want to get involved, but I didn't think it was.

It has turned out to work very well, we did one very simple thing, really. It's been a lot of work, I don't mean to make it sound simple, the team has done an amazing amount of work. We have a great editor and Marty Baron is a great publisher and Fred Ryan is a great technical leader. We've got a killer team at the Post, but the big kind of strategic change at the Post was flipping it from being a fantastic local regional newspaper to being a fantastic national global newspaper. The reason we did that is very simple, the Internet took away so many gifts from newspapers, mostly the kind of local ad monopolies and so on, like the Internet just dissolved all of the gifts that newspapers had, but the one gift that it brought to the table for newspapers is almost free global distribution because you can do it digitally. We refocused on that, and we had to switch from making a relatively large amount of money per reader on a relatively small number of readers to a small amount of money per reader on a much larger number of readers. And that's what we've done.

Kenneth Hersh: In our time remaining a couple of quick ones. Whom do you emulate?

Jeff Bezos: Kind of role model? A bunch of people, I have been a Warren Buffett since my early 20s, I read the things he writes. CEOs today out there that I like getting business from, Jamie Dimon. If I were a big shareholder in JP Morgan Chase, I would just show up every Monday morning with, like pastries and coffee for Jamie, and I would be like, so you're happy? You're good? Because I think he's a terrific executive in a very complicated company. Same thing. Bob Iger at Disney, I think he is a superb executive. Some bring him pastries. There are a lot of healthy models. And then outside of that, I've had lots of role models throughout my life, my teachers at River Oaks Elementary School that you mentioned, I had my parents whom I talked about earlier. I didn't talk too much with my grandfather, but he was a gigantic influence in my life. I had the great good fortune because my mom was so young, my grandparents would take me every summer, starting at age four, to give her a break, for the whole summer. So I'd be with my grandparents on their ranch in Cotulla, Texas, which is halfway between San Antonio and Laredo. We lived in Houston and so we would make the five-hour drive out to Kotula.
They'd drop me off, spend a couple of days there, then they go back to Houston. I went every day to the ranch with my grandfather to help. Now a four-year-old boy on a ranch in

South Texas. It's not a lot of help, but I didn't know that, I thought I was helping. And then by the time I was 16, I actually was helping. I can suture up a prolapsed cow, I can fix windmills. My grandfather was so resourceful that he made his own veterinary needles, he would take a little piece of wire and pound it flat with a mosaic, an oxy-acetylene torch, and then drill a little hole through it. We did all of our own veterinary work, some of the cattle even survived. We had great fun out there, we built barns and welded things. He bought a desex caterpillar used bulldozer 1955 model for five thousand dollars was completely broke and the gears were stripped. We spent a whole summer repairing that, the first thing we had to do to repair it, was build a crane to take the gears out of the transmission. What I learned from watching him was just how resourceful he was. He never called a repairman, he figured it out. And I do think that that's one of the things super lucky for me, to grow up in that environment where you got to see resourcefulness and action. So my grandfather was a giant role model for me.

Kenneth Hersh: Jeff, you are an American icon. And these stories really reflect how grounded you are, and starting a company from the time where you were doing it yourself, to where you are today. And to maintain that touch that you have, at the same time that you have this vision, is really what leadership is all about.

Air Force Association's Cyber Conference

(2018)

Talk with retired Gen. Larry Spencer at the conference in National Harbor, Md., in front of an Air Force audience:

Spencer: I have a wife who spends a lot of money, and I live in the D.C. area, and I could be looking for a job soon. So, any announcement you want to make about the headquarters?

Bezos: We'll make a decision before the end of the year. That's all I can say on that topic. We're excited to make that decision. And I hope your wife is spending some of that money on Amazon

Spencer: Oh, absolutely. One of the reasons we're happy to have you is that you are right in the wheelhouse of everything that's been going on here in the last few days, especially as we talk about innovation. If anyone epitomizes innovation, it's you and your companies. How do you encourage employees to be innovative? We've talked a lot here about the "frozen middle," how folks will have ideas and they can't get them through. A lot of folks worry about the risk: "What's going to happen if I make a mistake?" How do you encourage your employees to be innovative?

Bezos: This is a fantastic and important question. To be innovative you have to experiment. If you want to have more invention, you need to do more experiments per week, per month, per year, per decade. It's that simple. You cannot invent without experimenting. And here's the other thing about experiments: Lots of them fail. If you know it's going to work in advance, it is not an experiment.

What happens in big organizations — and Amazon is a big organization now, the Air Force is a big organization, is that we start to confuse experimentation with operational excellence. Operational excellence is one of our four key principles at Amazon. We've built over 150 large fulfillment centers around the world now. We know how to do that. That is not an experiment. If we build the 151st fulfillment center and screw it up, that's just a failure.

That's not the kind of failure we're seeking. We want failures where we're trying to do something new, untested, never proven. That's a real experiment. And they come at all scale sizes. So you need to teach people that those two kinds of failure are different.

You said something about that "hard middle," where ideas don't go up. I think this is such an important thing. At Amazon, one of the things we try to do is have multiple paths to "yes."

Here's a little thought experiment for you. If you are a junior executive at Amazon, and if Amazon did this in the typical kind of corporate hierarchy way, let's say you have an idea: You need to get your boss to greenlight that idea, and then your boss's boss needs to greenlight that idea. And then your boss's boss's boss needs to greenlight that idea. There are probably five levels or more before that idea gets the go-ahead.

Assume instead that you're an entrepreneur with a startup company idea, and you need venture capital. You go to Sand Hill Road [in Silicon Valley], and you go to the first venture capitalist and they tell you "no." You go to the second one, and they tell you "no." Maybe your 20th one tells you yes. You've got 19 no's and one yes, and you're still good to go.

In that venture capital model, there are multiple paths to yes. There were 20 people who could give you a yes, and it didn't matter how many gave you a no. So if you want innovative thinking, hire a large number of high judgment people empowered to greenlight ideas. You want multiple paths to yes. You want a system where, as a junior Air Force officer with a good idea, the first five people tell me no, but somehow I can still go pursue that idea.

That's a challenge that big organizations have to figure out. And by the way, this happens all the time: I'll say, "I don't think that's a good idea," but somebody else will greenlight it. I'm fine with that, because usually the cost of the experiments is pretty small.

Things only get expensive when they work, right? Once something works, you're like, "Whoa, we need to double down on that." Then the spending can get heavy, and then those can become big, consequential decisions. That's where the hierarchy and using the judgment of the most senior people really helps.

You also have to select people who like to invent. When you're in your hiring and your promotions process, you need to say,

"Does this person like to be innovative? Do they have a bit of the pioneering spirit?" Maybe they're also a little bit annoying because they might be, you know, a little bit radical or a bit of a rebel. They're not always the easiest people to get along with, but you want them in your organization.

They're a spice. I wouldn't recommend having 90 percent mavericks.

Spencer: What I found, at least in my military career, is that often mavericks, as you mentioned, are not welcomed. One of the phrases I really didn't like when I came up in the Air Force was "If it ain't broke, don't fix it." That doesn't mean you shouldn't make it better.

Bezos: Yeah. And by the way, your adversaries may be making it better.

Spencer: Exactly. So how do you handle these mavericks, and how do you protect them from the institution destroying them?

Bezos: You have to teach the value that these people bring. But also I would push hard on the mavericks to say, you also have to be organized. You can't just be a crazy person. It's fine to be a maverick, but write your ideas down. Sell your ideas. Persuade. Create the conditions where the ideas can blossom. If you're just purely a creative person with zero organizational skills, you're probably not going to get much done. So I would push back on the organization and say, look, these people have an important role to play.

By the way, all of us are a little bit of a maverick. It's not like there are these people who were born mavericks. We all have this inside of us. If you look at kids, they're all inventive. They're all doing crazy things.

I actually saw one of my kids put a square peg in a round hole, and as he was doing it, I would say "that's never going to work." And then it fit, and I was like, "Gosh, that's amazing."

Little kids try things. We all do that when we're little, and some of us lose it.

One of the great paradoxes of inventing at a high level is that you need to be an expert in your domain area, and you need to have a beginner's mind. You absolutely need both of those things. The world is too complex to actually just be a beginner.

No matter how inventive I am, I can't go invent a new kind of brain surgery. You have to be a neurosurgeon. You have to already know all there is to know about brain surgery, and then take it to the next level.

The problem is, for many people, by the time they become true experts, they've lost that ability to see things in a fresh way. They've lost the beginner's mind. And so that's another thing: If I'm an expert in launch vehicles or whatever it is, I need to step back and say, OK, if I were looking at this for the first time, what would I be seeing?

Spencer: For roughly 80 percent of my career in the Air Force, we would launch satellites and not think twice about it. Space was considered a sanctuary. Obviously, that has changed. So what do you see as the biggest challenges or risks in operating in the space domain?

Bezos: Let's start with a fundamental principle. You never want a fair fight. That's for a boxing ring. Outside of a boxing ring, a fair fight is just bad strategy. It means you didn't prepare properly. As you pointed out, this nation has enjoyed incredible space dominance for so long, but it's changing because some of our potential adversaries are getting very sophisticated.

If I were in your shoes, the way I would think about this is, in this new era, how are we going to maintain space dominance? What does it really mean? You're going to need some fundamental capabilities. You have to be able to go to space more frequently, with less lead time.

If you said, "Jeff, I have a mission for you. I need you to control this piece of terrain over here, but there are some constraints: You can only visit it once a month, with a lead time of two years," I've just been given an impossible mission.

So it's not surprising that it's difficult to do that. One of Blue Origin's missions is to make access to space more frequent, ready to go on a moment's notice, lower cost — which requires reusability. All those things are going to be required, in my view, to move into a new era of U.S. space dominance. And believe me, I don't have to tell you guys, you do not want to see that era end. That's a big deal.

Spencer: We have a lot of industry partners here in the audience. What are some of the benefits for your companies partnering with commercial industry?

Bezos: It's so important for the DOD, for the Air Force, for every government institution, when they can, to use commercial solutions. What I find is that when the requirements get written, they're not written necessarily taking that into account in all cases. And so you end up getting a custom-built system which meets the requirements, when a commercial system would have met a different set of requirements in a much better way for the capability that's required.

That's a big problem. It's very costly. It slows you down. You want to reserve your custom requirements for things where you really need special sauce. Something where there really isn't and shouldn't be a commercial avenue.

On writing requirements, I tell our engineers at Blue Origin: "Good engineers build to requirements. Great engineers push back on requirements." You need to say, "Is this requirement really needed? Because if we can waive this requirement, then we can use this commercial system."

If you look at an example from my own world, which is Amazon Web Services, we're now seeing fantastic growth from both companies and government institutions, the CIA, the DOD, using our compute cloud instead of building their own systems. And the reason these companies are doing that is because the capabilities they get keep improving, kind of automagically, without any effort. Part of what's going on there is, in a system like that, you want co-customers because the co-customers drive the product forward.

If you're the only customer of a software system, you're the only one driving it forward. If thousands customers share that system, then the other 999 that are not you are also driving it forward, and you get that as a tailwind.

The analogy I'll give you is that of a personal physician. The last thing you want, Larry, is a personal physician who only services you, because that person sure, they'd be available, they'd show up and do house calls, they'd be there anytime. But you want a doctor who's seeing hundreds of sick people so that when you have a problem that doctor has a bunch of data points.

How could a personal, private physician ever diagnose something? It would be so challenging. You don't want a private doctor, you want a bunch of co-patients, because those patients are teaching that doctor every day. If you can use a commercial system, you effectively have a doctor who has lots of patients teaching,

Spencer: Let's get specific about the Air Force. How would you recommend fostering innovation specifically with an organization like the Air Force, and with velocity?

Bezos: Velocity is so important, and in large organizations, it is about decision-making. What you really want is scale and nimbleness, right? So if you take the U.S. Air Force, one way to make it nimbler would be to make it much smaller, but that's a really bad solution because the scale brings so many advantages.

I see the same thing at Amazon. Because of our scale, we can do things that we just couldn't ever have done as a garage startup. There are some things that only big organizations can do. I love garage startups. I *was* a garage startup. But you can't build a Boeing 787 in your garage. You need a big organization like Boeing to do that.

So we want scale, we love scale, and you would never trade the scale of the U.S., Air Force for anything. But the question becomes, "How do I keep the advantages of scale but still have the advantages of a nimble startup? How do I get the nimbleness, too? I want to be able to absorb a punch because of my scale, and I want to be able to dodge a punch because of my nimbleness."

The way to stay nimble is by making decisions fast. In a 20-person startup company, the decision-making speed is so quick. That's why they're so nimble. In a big company or a big organization like the Air Force, that decision-making has a tendency to lose speed.

I'm the chief slowdown officer. I say, 'No, I want to see this one more way,' and the team that's working on it rolls their eyes.

You get high-quality decisions. I think sometimes people think the decisions are low-quality. You just get them slowly, which is a problem. This is what we do at Amazon: We acknowledge that there are two types of decisions. There are decisions that are "two-way doors." If you make the decision, you walk through the door, and if it turns out you made the wrong decision, you turn around, come back, and the consequence of that misstep is small.

That's a Type 2 decision. There's a Type 1 decision, where it's really hard to reverse course once you walk through that door. It's going to be expensive or impossible and time-consuming to reverse that decision, so you have to get that right. That's a high-consequence decision. Those decisions should be made deliberately, carefully, slowly.

At Amazon, I find myself on those decisions. I'm the chief slowdown officer. I slow those decisions down. I say, "No, I want to see this one more way," and the team that's working on it rolls their eyes. I've already seen it 18 ways, but I thought of a 19th way and I want to see it. That's correct. For a high-consequence, irreversible decision, you owe it to your teammates to make those decisions.

The problem that comes in with large organizations is that junior executives — I'll switch it to "officers" — junior officers see senior officers as their role models. So they're looking around and watching, and it turns out — rightly — that senior officers are mostly making high-consequence, Type 1 decisions that require a slow, deliberate decision-making process. So then the junior officers are like, well, that must be how we should make all decisions.

So now even trivial decisions end up going through a lot of extra unnecessary processes to be made. Really, many of those decisions should be made by very small teams, or even by single individuals with good judgment, knowing full well that they can be reversed.

Senior leadership can set the tone on that. They can say, "Why are so many people involved in this decision? I want Jill to make this decision, and whatever Jill decides is fine. And guess what, Jill, if you get it wrong, it's OK. We're just going to back up and do it again. I don't want you to talk to anybody about this. Just go make the decision."

Spencer: So I've been here in the hotel since last Thursday, and I decided to run home quickly last night to change out some clothes. Typical of my wife, I walked in the door after being gone for several days, and she asked me to take out the trash.

Bezos: She saved it for you.

Spencer: She did, but I didn't want to take out the trash. So I was considering OK, she asked me to take out the trash. Now, what's the risk to me by not taking it out?

Bezos: Over a beer, I want to hear how this ended up.

Spencer: The Air Force was birthed on innovation, so you have a generally innovative crowd here. However, there is a balance between innovation and risk. How do you balance those two?

Bezos: Well, here's what I would say: When you're doing these experiments, winners pay for thousands of losers. To put it in Amazon terms, we've had a few gigantic winners at Amazon. We've had Amazon Prime, our membership program. Amazon Web Services has been a gigantic winner. Our Marketplace business, where we let third-party sellers compete against us on our primary retail real estate. Those are huge winners for Amazon. Each of those winners has more than paid for thousands of experiments.

So when you're talking about the kinds of experiments that you would be doing here at the Air Force that I do at Amazon and Blue Origin, the positive outcome is very long tail. There's an analogy in baseball. Everybody knows that if you swing for the fences, you're going to hit more home runs, but you're also going to strike out more. In baseball, the most runs you can score when you're up at the plate is four. Your upside is capped. It's not long tailed. But in business, and I bet it's true here at the Air Force as well, that upside isn't really capped. Every once in a while, in business, you step up to the plate, you swing as hard as you can, and you get a thousand runs.

That long-tail distribution of those possible outcomes is what makes experimenting worthwhile. When you're balancing the risks, you say, "The most I can lose is the cost of the experiment, and the value of the invention could be uncapped."

Spencer: We obviously live in a very diverse world, a very diverse country and a very diverse Air Force. What role does diversity play in innovation? Not just race, ethnicity or gender, but also background?

Bezos: I think all of those types of diversity play a role in invention and innovation.The kind of invention that I see every day is team invention.

Amazon's Echo speaker with Alexa is an example of an invention that no customer asked for. If we had gone to customers, six years ago or seven years ago, and we said, "Look, would you buy a black cylinder that you plug into the wall in your kitchen, and you can ask it what time it is, set timers, ask it what the weather is, ask it to play music for you," they would have said, "No, I will not buy that."

So, we invented that. But there was no single person who invented it. It was team invention. People come at these things because of their diverse backgrounds — which I think does include gender and race and everything else, but also certainly "Did you come from a wealthy family? Did you come from a broken home?" All these things lead people to think in slightly different ways. And so when you do that team invention, you want people in the room thinking very differently. You're going to end up with a more robust invention.

Spencer: When you recruit folks for your company, and you mentor folks in your company, how are you recruiting and mentoring and raising the next Jeff Bezos?

Bezos: Well, it depends on the seniority of the person you're talking about. I teach a senior leaders class at Amazon, which I enjoy, and there I teach a bunch of different things. One of the things that really resonates with the folks I teach there is stress management. I offer to people that it's part of their job to make sure that they don't get burned out. I'm a member of the Business Council, and I meet with lots of other Fortune 500 CEOs from time to time. And I often hear them talking about how stressed they are. There seems to be this idea that the more senior you are, the more stress you should have. I think that's the opposite, because the more senior you are, the more control you have over your environment.

To a large degree, you get to pick who your senior staff is. To a large degree, you get to pick your schedule. To a large degree, you get to decide how you interact: Do you like to do lots of one-on-ones, or do you like to have small-group meetings? As a senior leader, you have a lot of control. And what I find is sometimes people forget that they have that control as a senior executive or as a senior officer. They forget that they can construct to a certain degree their work environment every day.

One of the things I try to do is preserve some time that's unscheduled, because I realized several years ago that hard work never stresses me out, but being overscheduled does stress me out. So I started working on ways that I can be less scheduled. I want to have a series of meetings that are just on standby that I can do whatever I want.

If you're working 60 hours a week, that's completely sustainable for most people, and if you're burned out by that, it's not the number of hours. You're doing something wrong.

Most speaking engagements that I do, I say, "I can't do it unless I can tell you the day before. If I can tell you the day before, there's probably a 50 percent chance or better than I can do it, but I don't want to let you down by canceling. And if I put this in my schedule, I know by the time the date arrives, I'm going to regret it either way."

The weird thing that happens when I do that is, I find I'm really excited to say yes and to go do it. It's just kind of human nature that you don't want to be forced into things. You want to know that it's your choice. And so, senior leaders have more choice.

The other thing that I try to teach in that regard is, I get asked by people in all age ranges, all levels of seniority, what do I think about work-life balance? My view on work-life balance is that I prefer the phrase "work-life harmony." To me, "balance" implies a strict tradeoff. And I have seen situations where people have all the time in the world, maybe they're out of work, and they're so stressed that they're actually terrible at home. Everybody at home is like, "Boy, I sure wish you'd get a job."

My sister-in-law says, "For better, for worse, but not for lunch."

So you really want harmony. They call it work for a reason. It's not going to be fun all the time. That's a pipe dream. None of us enjoys every minute of every day. And to have that kind of idea would just be naive. But there should be fun at work. You should be laughing. There should be moments of joy, and if you're getting energy from work instead of your work draining your energy, then you're going to come home and you're going to be a better mother, a better father, a better wife, a better husband.

You're going to want to take out the trash even before being asked. That's what's going to happen, Larry, your wife is just going to say, "Who is this guy?"

So if you're starting to get to the point where you are worried about work-life balance, I would challenge you to think it's just something out of whack. It's probably not the hours.

Look, if you're working 120 hours a week, you're also doing something wrong. That's too much. It's not sustainable. Maybe you can do that for a week or two, but that's it. But if you're working 60 hours a week, that's completely sustainable for most people, and if you're burned out by that, it's not the number of hours. You're doing something wrong. You need to figure out what it is, because you're going to take that home and then your home life is going to be stressful. And then you're bringing that back into the office, so it's going to be a negative spiral. That spiral will also be a positive one as soon as you turn it around.

Spencer: Now, I've only known you for a few minutes, but just talking to you in the green room, it's obvious that you like to have fun. So how do you create fun for your company, for folks who work for you?

Bezos: First of all, I think that the work itself should be fun. It's also great to layer on fun. If I think about the people that I work with, we have dinners together, we have Super Bowl parties together, we have impromptu concerts together. We do a lot of fun things, but the real thing is, when you're in a meeting and you're going through the important topics of the day or the year or the decade, whatever you're working on. Is that fun? You know, there are these people, when they walk in the room, they bring energy. That person walks in the meeting and everybody gets a little lift. Those people are worth their weight in gold.

And by the way, there is another kind of person who, when they walk into a meeting, you feel it. As soon as they walk in the room, it's very deflating. Everybody is like, uhhh. Don't be that guy. Figure out how to be the first guy, the person who when you enter the room, everybody is kind of excited. It's not that hard.

Every meeting should start with some encouragement and end with some encouragement. You can tell people very candid truths in the middle of the meeting, things they don't like and don't want to hear, but you can end it on an up note. You can also just say, "Look, we screwed this up, and we all know it." Even that can be fun if you acknowledge it. We screwed this up, we all know it, let's figure out how. Let's find the root cause. I believe in root causes, finding root causes, fixing root causes. Slow is smooth, and smooth is fast. Everything I've ever succeeded at in life is because of that philosophy.

Spencer: There are a couple of things that are certain in life. We've all heard about death and taxes, but there's a third certainty that I'm pretty confident about, and that's that your bank account is quite a bit larger than mine. Not much keeps me up at night, but what keeps you up at night?

Bezos: Well, I sleep extremely well. Even when I'm worrying over issues, it doesn't stop me from sleeping. I'm a gifted sleeper. But I know the way in which you mean the question. Amazon is such a big company now. It's grown so quickly.

I started the company in 1995. We opened our doors 23 years ago. I was delivering all the packages to the post office myself. I don't know if you know anything about my personal background. I was not born with a silver spoon in my mouth. My mother was pregnant with me in high school in Albuquerque, New Mexico and believe me, in 1964, it was not cool to be pregnant in high school. My grandfather went to bat for her. They tried to kick her out of high school, and my grandfather said, "You can't do that. It's a public school. She gets to finish high school."

The principal finally capitulated, but he said his terms were that my mom could not do any extracurricular activities or have a locker. My grandfather said, "OK, done, we'll take that deal." So she finished school.

Senior leaders need to be broken records on the things that are important to the organization.

My dad is a Cuban immigrant, and like most immigrants, he loves this country even more than those of us who were born here. And so I started this company, and I'm driving the packages to the post office myself. My big dream was that we would one day be able to afford a forklift. It was a tiny, tiny company.

Today it's almost 600,000 people. It's a very large company. And so the answer to your question, you know, metaphorically what keeps me awake at night, I worry about somehow losing our way with respect to our culture. Our culture is four things: customer obsession instead of competitor obsession; willingness to think long-term, with a longer investment horizon than most of our peers; eagerness to invent, which of course goes hand-in-hand with failure; and then, finally, taking professional pride in operational excellence.

The professional pride part is so important, because 90 percent of what all of you do, nobody ever sees. It's something that's inside the work. People see something finished, but they don't see what's inside it. Only you see that while you're doing the work. Nobody's going to be inspecting it. You're not going to get any credit for it. The only thing that's going to make you have high standards on that piece of the work that nobody's ever going to see is your own professional pride in operational excellence.

Those are the four cultural attributes that are used at Amazon. We use the same ones at Blue Origin, we use the same ones at AWS. If those things start to erode at the edges, that would make me very nervous. So I spend a lot of time trying to inspect that, audit that, teach that. Teaching things like that is about repetition. Senior leaders need to be broken records on the things that are important to the organization. You have succeeded when you start to see people roll their eyes because of your repetition on certain important things.

Senior leaders don't have to do a lot of things. They have to pick a few big ideas, and enforce tough execution against those big ideas. That requires a lot of repetition.

Bezos narrates a short video about Blue Origin's New Glenn rocket: New Glenn is our orbital vehicle. It has 3.85 million pounds of thrust. In terms of thrust, it's about half the size of a Saturn V. There are six landing gears, so we have landing-gear-out capability. The booster is fully reusable. It lands down range on a ship. It's powered by seven BE-4 engines. The BE-4's each have 550,000 pounds of thrust, and they're powered by liquefied natural gas and liquid oxygen.

We switched the second stage to liquid hydrogen using our BE-3U engine. Now the booster is coming back in for a landing. We've designed the landing ship to be underway so we can stabilize it really well, because we want to be able to land that booster even in heavy sea state.

There's a big team of people working very hard to make all of that come true in the very near future. Next year I will invest just over a billion dollars in that program.

Bezos narrates a video about the BE-4 rocket engine: It uses oxidizer-rich staged combustion. The test program is going very well, the team's doing a great job.

Bezos narrates a video recap of July's uncrewed test flight of Blue Origin's New Shepard suborbital spaceship: This will be putting people in space this coming year. This was our third envelope test of the escape system. The system uses a solid rocket motor with 70,000 pounds of thrust that takes the crew capsule away from the booster. This particular test was the high-altitude escape test. We were basically already in space. Just before the main engine cutoff is when this would happen in real life. It's one of the more stressing cases. Watching this landing never gets old for me.

Bezos shows a drone's-eye view of Blue Origin's New Glenn rocket factory and launch facility in Florida: This is a 650,000-square-foot manufacturing facility. It's up and operating now. As far as I know, we're one of the only launch companies actually building a manufacturing facility right there on the Space Coast. We leased Launch Pad 36 at Cape Canaveral. Between these two facilities, the manufacturing facility and Pad 36, we've already invested about a billion dollars in the Space Coast.

One of the reasons I like to talk about how much we've invested is, I do want people, especially this audience, to know how committed we are. We're in.

Spencer: My final question is, at the end of the day, in the Air Force, we're about leadership. Most people will never get to be CEO of a major company. You're the CEO of multiple companies. So what two or three leadership principles have really helped you manage large organizations?

Bezos: There are a bunch of them. I mentioned one of them earlier, which I think is the most important thing. If you're really talking about the most senior leader, the most senior leader has to know what the big ideas are for their organization. At Amazon, I know what the big ideas are: low prices, fast delivery, and vast huge selection. Those are the three big ideas, and those ideas are permanent. Because they're never going to change, we can put energy into them, and the energy we put in today is going to be paying dividends later. It's impossible to imagine,10 years from now, that somebody in this room will come to me and say, "Jeff, I love Amazon. I would just wish you charged slightly higher prices." Or: "I love Amazon. I just wish you'd deliver a little more slowly."

Same thing with Blue Origin. I know what customers want. The big ideas are so obvious: lower cost, higher availability, more reliability. It needs to work every time. It needs to fly when you say you're going to fly. And it needs to be way cheaper.

The great thing about the big ideas is you don't have to launch a research project to figure them out.

Once you identify those big things, then you can build strategies around each of them. What's the strategy around low cost? It's reusability. And by the way, it has to be real reasonability, like New Shepard. That vehicle is designed for actual operational reusability. We don't take the thing apart and inspect it between flights. We fly it over and over. If you build a space vehicle that you have to inspect in an intense way and disassemble and refurbish between flights, that's going to be more expensive than an expendable vehicle. It has to be real operational resilience.

So what's the strategy for New Glenn on reliability? Well, one of them is one-fault operative. Our entire architecture uses a one-fault operative requirement. What about availability? There's a bunch of things: I showed you the landing ship being stabilized underway, so that we don't have to worry about the sea states downrange. There are others, too. We have a requirement in New Glenn that launch shall not be delayed by anyone sensor being out. So if we have one sensor out, that should not affect availability.

Basically, once you identify the big ideas, you keep iterating on them and asking the team, "What more can we do for availability?" AWS has the same thing. Everybody who does cloud computing, what do they want? They want data security. Nobody's going to say, "Well, I wish my data was just a little less secure." They also want availability. They don't want their service to be down.

The great thing about the big ideas is you don't have to launch a research project to figure them out. You know what they are in your head already. That's how big they are. All you have to do is talk about them a lot and make sure that the whole organization is putting energy into them.

Spencer: Great. Well, Jeff, thank you so much. I can't tell you how much we appreciate you being here.

Bezos: I'd just like to make one more remark, which is: In life, you can have a job, you can have a career, or you can have a calling. And if you have a calling, you've really made it. And I believe most of the people in this room have really made it, because what you're doing has meaning, and that matters. And I just want to thank you for that. I love it.

Chat in Mumbai
with Actor Shah Rukh Khan and Filmmaker Zoya Akhtar
(2020)

Shah Rukh Khan: Tell me have you seen any perceptible change in India apart from the traffic, when you came last?

Jeff Bezos: Apart from the traffic. You know it's interesting. So, I guess the first time I came to India was about 11 years ago. I don't know that I have seen perceptible changes of integrate magnitude. The thing what I would actually say is that, I notice there are certain things that seem to me to be the same and I love those things. One of the things I notice every time I come here is that, there is so much energy here, dynamism and color. The word I would use for it is, the whole place seems so full of life everywhere you go every single thing you do, and the diversity of India.

When I come here, I've never seen a more diverse place. Everywhere I travel in the world nowhere more diverse than India. So, the energy, self-improvement. Every time I come here, I find that the people that I talk to are focused on and interested in being better tomorrow than they are today. Everybody here seems to be focused on self-improvement. So I when I get here I get a boost of energy.

Zoya Akhtar: Did you think online retail would get this big?

Jeff Bezos: Oh no. You know when I started Amazon, it was 25 years ago, I started Amazon in 1994. When I went to see investors, the first question I had to answer was, what is the internet? None of my investors had ever heard of the internet. The idea I had in mind was to build a bookstore. I realized that we could build a store, which would have every book ever printed in any language, in print or out of print and we could do that online. It would be impossible in a physical store and that was the founding idea of amazon.

But did I expect what would happen today? No, I've been at Amazon when it was one person, me. When it was 10 people when it was a hundred people when it was a thousand people. And today it's, as you know, more than 700,000 people and approaching 70,000 people just here in India. So, no I did not predict that and actually I think if anybody had predicted that they would have needed to be immediately institutionalized in a mental facility. Because it's not a normal thing to have happened. My dream when I started Amazon was that one day, we might be able to afford a forklift. So, it's been a very fun journey for me, and by the way I still tap dance into work. I'm having so much fun.

Zoya Akhtar: Is there anything you don't sell on Amazon?

Jeff Bezos: Anything we don't sell?

Zoya Akhtar: Or anything you tried to sell and didn't work? Anything that you decided not to go?

Jeff Bezos: There are things we tried to sell that didn't work, we tried to sell a phone, call the Fire Phone. We worked on it for four years and no one bought it. I think my mother bought one and I don't think she was that happy with it. But no, there are things that we deliberately don't sell. We don't sell guns; we don't sell tobacco. There are things we don't sell, but that we make deliberate decisions about. But other than those things we try to sell everything that anyone might want to buy and we're trying to make it as convenient as possible for people. You know in the early 21st century we're all busy. Everybody in this room is busy, and if you can save people's time and let them spend more time with their families and their friends and doing the things that they really enjoy, then you're doing them real service.

Shah Rukh Khan: Most of the people here Jeff, are from the film industry. It was very heartening when Amazon started creating original content. So, we don't think of our films as just products, there's a very clear demarcation. You know, some of them think, 'We do a film for the creative fun of it, for the artistry of it.' Or this one is for business. We don't look down upon it, but we clearly demarcate it. Now that you are into original content in a big way. What's your stance on it? Are you still that person who says, no? I'm going to do this for the creativity, the artistry, forget the business, or I'm doing this only for the business? Or, is it a mix of both, and you say just put on lots of stuff let someone come on the story and find whatever they want?

Jeff Bezos: I think this is a great question. It's actually something we debate, I think, if you look at the very best things in the world, they do both. I think this is a golden age of television. When you look at your TV series today, the really good TV series are in terms of quality, they're as good as the very best movies have ever been. And you know, you're getting the best storytellers to come to television, you're getting the best actors to now come do television. We're are now one of the great storytellers.

Zoya Akhtar: Thank you.

Jeff Bezos: And this is a big deal. When you can get the very best people, because this is one of those businesses where the viewer is always looking for something a little fresh. And so, you can never find a formula, because as soon as you find a formula it's not fresh anymore. They're always looking for something a little new. So, it really takes human ingenuity; the storytellers have to be in touch with the zeitgeist. I want Amazon studios to be all over the world, I want us to be known as the most talent friendly studio in the world.

The reason you need to do that, is because at the end of the day it is the talent that makes those stories. Storytelling is the oldest thing that humans do. We've been doing it for thousands and thousands of years long before there was written language before there was any medium to convey it. People sat around and they told each other stories, and it's how we teach each other things. We learn from stories, we learn from fiction. We learn from fiction because we get to live an alternate life, in that moment you watch this and you're learning.

So, it can be fun, it can be action, it can be funny, it can be comedy. But the very best thing is to take those elements and teach a little something. There's something in there that you walk away with and you're inspired by it. It doesn't matter if it's drama, comedy, anything, you're going to walk away with something and there needs to be lightness. You know you can't watch something that's just all heavy and you're like, 'Oh my God, I want to kill myself now.' There also has to be that gesture there has to be somebody who brings you out and lets you breathe a little bit. And this is so hard to do.

That's why there are so many bad movies and so many bad TV shows. Because it is one of the hardest things that humans do, is tell riveting, engaging, inspiring stories. But when you get it right, it's a lever that can change the world.

Zoya Akhtar: Are you a competitive producer?

Jeff Bezos: Am I what?

Zoya Akhtar: A competitive producer and I don't mean business wise; I mean creatively. Like, would you see a film or a show on another platform, like what you described which is brilliant and be like, 'why don't I have this?'

Jeff Bezos: Well, I have regrets. I mean we've turned down things that later were so good. I wish we hadn't turned them down. But we've also picked up things that other people turned down and we've made them great. So, the truth is storytelling is infinite. If I tell a good story, it doesn't make your story bad. These are not substitute products, you know. I don't feel like you get the best results with storytelling by trying to make sure that other people's stories are worse than your stories. There can be a lot of good stories in the world.

You're really competing not against others, you're competing against this.

That's why, you guys have all seen this. If you're in the entertainment business, there are movies and TV shows where you know the people involved, and every one of those people is talented, and still the final product is bad, it happens. And because there's a little bit of mystery to it, we don't know how to do it perfectly. That's what makes it so fun.

Shah Rukh Khan: Is there something you think is a sheer waste of time?

Jeff Bezos: Look there are a lot of things that are a waste of time. When you think about your life, I think I often tell people that I work with, because people have very high standards for how they want their work life to be. I say, look, if you can get your work life to be where you enjoy half of it, that is amazing. Because very few people ever achieve that, because the truth is everything comes with overhead. That's reality, everything comes with pieces that you don't like. You could be a supreme court justice and there's still going to be pieces of your job you don't like, or you can be a university professor and it's still going to be that you have to go to committee meetings. You know every job comes with pieces you don't like and we need to say, that's part of it. And not resent those pieces or try not to, but try to minimize them. I tell senior executives; you should have the least stress. You know there's this weird false idea that CEOs are under the most stress. Well, I look at that, I'm like why, you're in charge. Why don't you delegate the stress? It's your choice. So, you have to figure out how to set up your life in such a way that you can minimize these things.

I find people don't dislike hard work; what people dislike is being out of control. Like, they can't control their life, they can't control their environment. This happens to me when I get over scheduled. I hate being over scheduled. I want some time to be able to think and free myself, we all have the same amount of time in the world. Nobody has more time than anybody else. When you become a very successful person, one of the things you start to get is over scheduled. You have this event, you had to agree to do this and maybe last night you were like, 'why did I agree to do this?' I have to go on stage tomorrow, I wish I were really with my family. Let's say in general that kind of thing happens. So, you have to guard your time and try to say a little bit flexible. For me it's not a waste of time, but I like to have some freedom of movement rather than having every minute of every day scheduled.

Zoya Akhtar: What is your one hot tip for somebody on the onset of their career?

Jeff Bezos: So, a young person starting their career, I think there are probably a lot of things. Some of them are very well known and people have heard them many times they're still true. One of those that you should always focus, a young person should find something that they're passionate about to do. And that's not going to surprise anyone, it's a clear thing to do. It's very hard, if you don't love your work, you're never going to be great at it. I think the other thing I would suggest to any young person even before they start their career is to really think about their choices. I find that young people don't, when I was young I made this mistake too. You can get very fixed on your gifts, so everybody has gifts. You know you have gifts and you have things that you didn't get gifted. Maybe you're extremely beautiful, maybe you're extremely good at mathematics. Maybe you, there are a lot of things that you can be given. But those things can confuse you because they're not the things that construct your life. It's your choices that construct your life, not your gifts. You can celebrate your gifts; be proud of them be happy of them. Actually, don't be proud of them, be celebratory of them. You can't be proud because they're gifts, they were given to you, you didn't earn them.

You can only be proud of the things you earn, and so as I got older, I started to realize I wasn't proud of my gifts. I was always good at school, school was always easy for me and I was always proud that I was a great student. I got A's in all my classes; I was good at math and all of that. I thought that's who I was, but it's not true. Those are the things that are gifts, what was hard for me is deciding to work hard, deciding to use my gifts in certain ways. To challenge myself to do things that I didn't think I could do. To put myself in uncomfortable situations.

We all get, I would say to a young person you can choose a life of ease and comfort or you can choose a life of service and adventure. Which one of those when you're 90 years old, are you going to be more proud of?

Shah Rukh Khan: I want to know Jeff, is there a job, if it wasn't Amazon if it wasn't business related. Is there something else, if you started all over again at this age and stage and took on a different profession? Would there be one that is close to your heart?

Jeff Bezos: I would be very curious today, if I were a young college student today, I would be very interested in biotechnology. I think biotechnology is a just a fascinating arena that probably in the near in the next 10 or 20 years is going to be a golden age of biotech. One of the golden ages that's happening right now before our eyes is also artificial intelligence and machine learning. So, that's another arena that I would be very interested in. My backup career is I'm a very good bartender. So, if all else fails, you'll see me at the local bar, and I'll be making drinks slowly but they'll be good.

Zoya Akhtar: If there's one thing you could have more of, what would that be?

Jeff Bezos: One thing I could have more of, I mean the obvious answer is time. You know it is time to do, I like time. I'm not efficient with my time, the embedded assumption is that you know where you're going. I like to wander, because it's wandering that allows you to invent and to explore and to follow your curiosity. But wandering is very time consuming, and so if I could have one more thing it would just be more time.

Shah Rukh Khan: So, wonderful. A big round of applause for Jeff and for Zoya. Thank you so much."

Interview at the Aspen Institute

(2016)

Walter Isaacson: All right, that's where we'll start. Where did you get that laugh

Jeff Bezos: My laugh is something that I have had since I was the tiniest child. There was a time when my brother and sister would not go see a movie with me because it was too damn embarrassing. So anyway, it's there.

Walter Isaacson: Do you ever deploy it intentionally or is it only unintentional,

Jeff Bezos: Believe it or not? It's very difficult. I would make a great ethnic man. I could be somebody's sidekick, you know, sit there on the sofa and just laugh at all their jokes. And it would be very genuine. I turn out to be easily amused.

Walter Isaacson: That's good. So as number one on the list, we're talking to Steve Case yesterday and he had been number one. And a couple of years later, he was not on the list.

Jeff Bezos: Well, you're making me really nervous.

Walter Isaacson: No, no. Don't be nervous. Just tell me what could happen that would do that to you and Amazon. And how do you prevent that? Do you worry it could all come unraveled?

Jeff Bezos: Well, I kind of have this experience kind of already happened to me because you put me on the cover of TIME magazine's Person of the Year in 1999 and about a year later, the Internet bubble burst. I think Amazon stock went from one hundred and thirteen dollars a share to six or something like that. So, you know, the thing for companies is you need to be nimble and robust, so you need to be able to take a punch. You also need to be quick and innovative and doing new things at a high speed. That's the best defense against the future. You have to always be leaning into the future. If you're leaning away from the future, the future is going to win every time. Never, ever, ever lean away from the future.

Walter Isaacson: In 1999, when Jim Kelly, myself and others at Time chose you as Person of the Year, I remember the Internet bubble was beginning to look like it might burst. That November of 1999, I went up to Don Logan, who was then the president of Time Inc, somebody above us all. I said, look, I'm a little bit worried. We're about to do Jeff Bezos, it's an Internet company, you know, tell me what you think. He said, Jeff Bezos is not in the Internet business, he's in the customer service business, you don't have to worry. How did you get that focus on customer service rather than on being an Internet company?

Jeff Bezos: I don't know. I think we have always from the very, very beginning. You can go back and read our 1997 shareholder letter. The core of the company is customer obsession as opposed to competitor obsession. That works really well for us. It's I think that the advantage of being customer focused is that customers are always dissatisfied, they always want more, and so they pull you along. If you're trying to serve them, they pull you along. Whereas if your competitor obsessed, if you're a leader, you know, you can kind of look around and you see everybody running behind you. Maybe you slow down a little and customers are always pulling you. So I think if you want to be pioneering, if you want to be inventive, if you want a culture that is experimental, then you want to be customer obsessed rather than competitor obsessed.

Walter Isaacson: Now, how does something like Alexa and the Amazon Echo fit in to being customer obsessed?

Jeff Bezos: Well, it's definitely about leaning into the future. So when you look at the kinds of things that you want to be able to do with your voice, it changes for those of you who have used an echo, the fact that it's always on that you never have to charge it. It's always sitting there ready in your kitchen or your bedroom or wherever you put it. The fact that you can talk to it in an natural way, removes a lot of barriers, a lot of friction, a lot of like little tiny pieces of friction to be able to do things to ask what the weather is. It's easier than taking your phone out of your pocket and what people have found over and over again by removing the tiniest amounts of friction from ordinary activities. Really, people appreciate that and it improves customers lives.

Walter Isaacson: And does it learn?

Jeff Bezos: Yeah, it's always learning, the brains of Alexa are in the cloud. They're not on that little device. So that's why the device is actually as a physical device, relatively simple. It's the speaker has seven microphones that has enough digital signal processing power on board to be able to do beam forming. Find your voice, acknowledge the wake word. The wake word is Alexa, and then it starts listening and sends that phrase to the cloud where we can do real compute intensive processing on it.

Walter Isaacson: Here's a real paranoid question, because you just said Alexa is the wake word. Does it listen, if I don't say Alexa?

Jeff Bezos: No, it listens just for that word, and that's why we do the wake word detection locally on the device.

Walter Isaacson: Let's say I talk about toothpaste, but have mot said Alexa, it's not like Amazon is learning that I'm interested in toothpaste?

Jeff Bezos: Not at all. In fact, the you guys should you know, one of the great issues of our age is going to be privacy. And you know, people don't think about it, but if you have a mobile phone in your pocket, it has microphones on it and those microphones are under software control. I would posit to you that just about any nation state in the world worth its salt, can put a computer virus on your phone any time they want and listen to everything you say from your cell phone.

Walter Isaacson: How do you prevent that from happening to Echo?

Jeff Bezos: Well, we've done something a little unusual with Echo because we were thinking about that very thing. We first of all, we no different from your phone, but we actually went one step further than what's done on the phone. When you hit the mute button on Echo, that red ring comes on that says the microphone is turned off. That mute button is connected to the microphone with analog electronics. So it actually cannot be routed, you'd have to come physically tamper with the device. You couldn't do it with a computer virus.

Walter Isaacson: So it learns. And that got you into the artificial intelligence world, machine learning world so that you could get in cloud computing.

Jeff Bezos: We've been in the machine learning world for a long time. You know, we live in a very interesting time because there are a few golden ages happening and one of them is machine learning. It's kind of specialized A.I. We're doing everything with it. We're grading strawberries with it for Amazon Fresh with cameras that look at the strawberries and we can now outperform humans on strawberry grading. So I give you that tiny example to show you that artificial intelligence and machine vision and natural language understanding these kinds of amazing things that just 10 years ago were science fiction are going to be very helpful everywhere.

Walter Isaacson: You bought the Washington Post and at least the myth is you did it almost on a handshake without a whole lot.

Jeff Bezos: That's not a myth. I did zero due diligence, I did not negotiate. I accepted the asking price. it wouldn't have happened that way, except for the person that I was dealing with was Don Graham, who I've known for 15 years and who is the most honorable person in the world. We had several conversations and he laid out every single wart and every single thing that was great about the post. I would say, no due diligence would have ever uncovered the things that Don just told me, number one. And number two, I've owned the paper for a couple of years now. And if anything, the the words are not as bad as he made them out to be, and the things that are great about the post are stronger than he made them out to be. So how could I ever have duplicated that with some kind of due diligence process?

Walter Isaacson: You over the past two years talked about an emerging view of what a business model could be. Give me some of the thought of what a business model for The Washington Post could be in the next five years.

Jeff Bezos: It's I think very simple what we have to do at the Post from a business point of view. First of all, to make the post great is not our business model. What makes the post great is the tradition of investigative journalism and all the things that they have in the newsroom. I think the newsroom of the Post is absolutely killing it. I'm incredibly proud of that team. Marty Baron, in my opinion, is the best executive editor of any newspaper anywhere in the world. The culture of the Post is very unusual because they have a kind of swashbuckling, but they're like professional swashbucklers. You don't want just swashbuckling, without professionalism swashbuckling just gets you killed.

Walter Isaacson: How do they know that? do you hang in the newsroom?

Jeff Bezos: No, I don't. Well, I occasionally do. But hang would give you the wrong sense. I'm not there very often. I have a day job which I love. I tap dance into Amazon. I live on the other side of the country, literally. I call Washington, D.C., the other Washington. So it's not practical for me to be there all the time. But for example, I started to get a sense, a very powerful sense of it when I went to Ben Bradlee's funeral. So there's a long tradition of the Post of just putting a lot of shoeleather into things and finding stories that nobody else can find, and the Post is very lucky because it is physically located in the capital city of the most important country in the world. As a result, they have lots of contacts and lots of opportunities because of that physical location.

Walter Isaacson: You basically tied The New York Times to a digital and perhaps with your tape of Donald Trump and Billy Bush, that's probably not counted in yet. That'll take you way ahead of The New York Times. How do you monetize that?

Jeff Bezos: The politics team of the Post is just doing a great job this year, and I'm super proud of them. I don't know that this approach is accessible to all newspapers, but I'm very confident it is an approach that will work for the Post. But what we need to do is to move from making a relatively large amount of money per reader on a relatively small number of readers, that was the traditional Post model for decades, very successful model, by the way. We need to move from that to a model where we make a very small amount of money per reader on a much, much larger number of readers.

Walter Isaacson: That would require micropayment or small payments.

Jeff Bezos: I don't think so. I think we can do it with a combination of a subscription model and an ad model. We'll see. But I'd be open to micro payments.
But these things can change. I don't see evidence yet that consumers are amenable to those kinds of micro payments. But we've seen this change in the early days of music subscription service, consumers were not amenable to music subscriptions. They didn't want that. They wanted to buy music on a cart, today that's flipped around. And so habits, behaviors and patterns of consumers do change slowly over time. And maybe one day they will pay.

Walter Isaacson: You keep Amazon and the Post separate. Yet in your mind, that would be a connection between, all right, we should enable really frictionless 10, 15, 20 cent payments that could be done through Amazon, also through The

Washington Post. Do you ever see a world in which we're going to have those type of let me buy the paper today for 10 cents as opposed to subscribe?

Jeff Bezos: Again, I think it's possible. I'm currently a little skeptical about that. I think there's so much advertising supported news out there that it's maybe difficult to get people to pay 10 cents,

Walter Isaacson: Get back to the shoe leather. And the very beginning of this campaign, I think Bob Woodward talked a little bit about it, too. You decide to throw the kitchen sink and everything to a book on Donald Trump. How involved were you in that decision?

Jeff Bezos: Zero, that's Marty Barons decision? I do not introduce myself in any way into the daily activities of the newsroom. My view on that would be it would be a little bit like, I don't know. Let's say one of your children had to have an operation on their brain. Would you go into the operating theatre and tell the neurosurgeon what to do? This is a highly professionalized activity and we have people who have decades of experience doing it. I help or tried to help at a much higher level than should we we cover this story or that story. Marty just has an awesome team. They have good taste in these matters. That's really critical.

I did not hire Marty. Marty was there already again one of the things that Don Graham told me was great about the paper and he was right. Same thing with Fred Hiatt, who leads the editorial pages, Fred Ryan, who's the publisher, Shalash, who runs technology, a killer team.

Walter Isaacson: But one person who doesn't understand that you don't order up stories like that is Donald Trump. He's a very, very personal. And then you've had to answer him in the newsroom, or at least in discussions with watching both people. How do you respond to those attacks and what do you tell Donald Trump?

Jeff Bezos: So, you know, he's done a couple of times with me. He's done it with many people. I'm not unique by any means. But, you know, when he did it the first time, my instinct was to take it very lightly. In fact, I did take it lightly. I sent what I thought was a humorous tweet that had taken a hashtag send Donald to space. The final thing in the hashtag and you know, I have a rocket company, so, you know the capability is there and that was my initial take on this. Then the more I thought about it, that was a mistake. I should not have taken it lightly because, you know, we live in an amazing country where one of the things that makes this country so as amazing as it is, is that we are allowed to criticize and scrutinize our elected leaders. There are other countries where if you criticize the elected leader, you might go to jail or worse, you may just disappear. That is the appropriate thing for a presidential candidate to do is to say, I am running for the highest office in the most important country in the world. Please scrutinize me, please scrutinize me. That would, by the way, signal great confidence. It would be a leader thing to do. And, you know, that's not what we've seen. To try and show the media a sort of threaten retribution, retaliation, which is what he's done in a number of cases for people involved in the media, it just isn't appropriate. We have freedom of speech in this country. It's written into the Constitution. But the Constitution, except for our norms and our behaviors, the stories we tell ourselves as a nation about who we are, it's just a piece of paper. There are a bunch of nations that have written constitutions that they don't pay any attention to. People still disappear.

Walter Isaacson: Do you think that Donald Trump has crossed the line on the norm to be dangerous?

Jeff Bezos: He is eroding on issues like that? He is eroding. I don't know how dangerous that is because I think the United States is incredibly robust. We have you know, we are not a new democracy. We're very robust. But it is you know, it is inappropriate for a presidential candidate to erode that around the edges. They should be trying to burnish it instead of erode it. When you look at the pattern of things, it's not just going after the media, threatening retribution for people who scrutinize him. It is also, saying that he may not give a graceful concession speech if he loses the election. That erodes our democracy around the edges. You know, saying that he might lock up his opponent if he wins erodes our democracy around the edges. These aren't acceptable behaviors, my opinion.

Walter Isaacson: Well, thank you. And by the way, before we move on, I want to thank you in terms of The Washington Post, which has really hit it out of the park this year when it comes to political cover, things like that. Even if Marty deserves the credit, he does applaud.

Jeff Bezos: Yes, I will accept that compliment on behalf of the amazing team.

Walter Isaacson: I think we applauded Marty yesterday on this well earned that. Going back to artificial intelligence. Suppose I had Alexa and Siri sitting right here. What's the difference between the way they learn, the algorithms they use?

Jeff Bezos: Well, I don't know a lot about the internal operations of Siri, so it's hard for me to answer that. You know, Alexa uses the technique called deep learning, a lot of the new machine learning systems are using deep learning, at least as one element of what they're doing. And and she's continuously learning as she interacts with you, getting better, trying to understand not only your speech patterns, but also the kinds of things that you're interested in, things as simple as music, but more complicated things, too.

Walter Isaacson: Well, when I look at what you're doing in A.I. cloud machine learning space, whatever, it makes it seem like you're more of a science geek than a onto just a pure entrepreneur. I'm going to play biographer for just a little bit growing up. I know how wonderful your parents are. Ety And Mike, what was it that caught on to science? What gave you this background?

Jeff Bezos: I don't know. You don't get to choose your passions. Your passions choose you. I watched Neil Armstrong step on the moon when I was five years old, had a huge impact on me. I read, you know, hundreds of science fiction novels. By the time I was 12 or 13, I always liked science and math, went to Princeton to study physics and switching to computer science.

Walter Isaacson: Did you have a grandfather or a mother?

Jeff Bezos: You win a lot of lotteries in life and you lose some lotteries in life. One of the great lotteries that I won was role models. My mom, you know my parents my mom had me when she was 17 years old. She was pregnant in 1963 in Albuquerque, New Mexico, in high school, which was not cool and the principal tried to kick her out of school. My grandfather, we called him Pop. He went to bat for her and met with the principal and said, look, you can't kick her out of school. She's allowed to finish school and cut a deal with him. He said, well, she can stay and finish high school, but she can't have a locker and she can't do any extracurricular activities. My grandfather, being a very wise man, was like done hat will work. My dad is a Cuban immigrant. came over part of Operation Pedro Pan right after Castro took over, two weeks in Everglades refugee camp, picked up by a Catholic mission with 15 other Cuban boys. The Catholic Church took great care of him. So they both had their own remarkable lives. They are incredibly supportive of me and my brother and sister. So that's why they have you know, they're hard working. They care about things, they're supportive. My mom is the kind of mother who, you know, anything I do is amazing.

Jeff Bezos: You know, it's like, look, he made scrambled eggs and they're not dry, you know, that kind of thing. So that's a great to grow up in an environment like that is a gigantic lottery. I spent all my summers from maybe age 4 to 16 on my grandfather's ranch in south Texas and learning all kinds of things that you can only learn in a rural environment, rural people can be so self resourceful. You don't necessarily call a vet or call somebody to fix the air conditioning when it breaks, you figure out how to fix it yourself, it was really a great experience for me. I think my grandfather took me all the summers to give my mom a break. She was so young. We used to watch Days of our Lives together. My grandmother had died and my grandfather had always watch Days of our lives with my grandmother, and he remained addicted to it. During the hottest part of the day, at like one o'clock in the afternoon we would go back to the ranch house and watch Days of our Lives, like sands through an hourglass.

Walter Isaacson: Amazing, you also developed a love of space. And even in West Texas now, not too far from that ranch, you've been quite successful in the past month or so, shooting up things, why?

Jeff Bezos: Why space? or why are we doing this? So first, it's important, I think, and I can tell you why. But, what I want to achieve with Blue Origin is to build the heavy lifting infrastructure that allows for the kind of dynamic entrepreneurial explosion of thousands of companies in space that I have witnessed over the last twenty one years on the Internet. So when I think about the founding of Amazon.com, it only could work. So take you back to nineteen ninety five, July nineteen ninety five. We open our doors and this is a 10 person company. I'm driving the packages to the post office myself and. We were sitting on a bunch of heavy lifting infrastructure, otherwise a tiny company could never have started Amazon.com, you couldn't do it. For example, there was already a gigantic logistics network called the US Postal Service and UPS and FedEx that would have been tens of billions, actually hundreds of billions of dollars of capital that you would have had to have laid out if you had to build a logistics network. We didn't have to do that. It existed, the heavy lifting was already done. On the Internet itself was sitting on top of at that time, the long distance phone network. Again, tens of billions, hundreds of billions of dollars of capital put in place for long distance phone calls, but repurposed for the Internet. Payment system, there was already a payment system. We didn't have to do that. It was called the credit card and had been initially put in place for travelers and so on and so on.

Jeff Bezos: What we were able to do is take all of the heavy lifting infrastructure and kind of reassemble it in a new way and do something new and inventive with it. That's one lens through which you can view the founding of Amazon.com. In space today, that is impossible. On the Internet today, two kids in their dorm room can reinvent an industry. Because the lifting infrastructures are in place for that. Today, two kids in their dorm room, can't do anything interesting in space. You could build a CubeSat. There's not that much interesting about CubeSat. That may change. But right now, there's are certain laws of physics and certain things you need size for. Things need to be big. We need to be able to put big things in space at low cost. If I'm 80 years old and I can say to myself that Blue Origin did the heavy lifting, you know, I am using my Amazon winnings to do a new piece of heavy lifting infrastructure, which is low cost access to space, vehicles have to be reusable. You can't throw them away, throw away space vehicles every time, you're never going to lower the cost. So we're trying to lower the price of admission into space so that thousands of entrepreneurs can then do amazing, surprising things.

Jeff Bezos: Nobody in ninety five predicted Snapchat. You know, I can't predict for you what amazing entrepreneurs, brilliant, amazing entrepreneurs will do in space. But I know if I give them low cost access to space, some brilliant, twenty two year old is going to figure it out.

Walter Isaacson: It's one of those things about what companies get sustainable. It's those that provide platforms upon which others can build.

Jeff Bezos: If you empower others, empower others to do things. So AWS is like that, Kindle Direct Publishing is like that, third party selling businesses is like that, fulfillment by Amazon is like that. Every time you figure out some way of providing tools and services that empower other people to deploy their creativity, you're really on to something.

Axel Springer Award 2018

Mathias Döpfner, the CEO of Business Insider's parent company, Axel Springer, recently sat down with Amazon CEO Jeff Bezos to talk about the early days of creating Amazon, what he's learned since then, how he funds his rocket company, Blue Origin, and what it's like when the president of the United States is your biggest critic.

Mathias Döpfner: Jeff, welcome to Berlin.

Jeff Bezos: Thanks. It's great to be here.

Döpfner: When we were sitting in the first row just a couple of minutes ago, waiting for the award ceremony, you looked at me: "Mathias, are you nervous?" And I said, "Yes, I'm always nervous on occasions like this." And you said, "So am I." And I said, "Really? The richest person in the world is nervous . . . ."

Jeff, you used to work in New York as an investment banker. So, an investment banker is actually the exact opposite of an entrepreneur. He's not taking risks himself, he is taking advantage of risks that other people take. How did you dare to think that you should become an entrepreneur and really launch a company?

Bezos: I think I always wanted to do it, even since I was a kid. I had the idea. I was one of those people who every time I looked at something it looks like it could be improved, there's something wrong with it. So I'd go through, like, how could this restaurant be better? So I've always had that kind of idea.

By the way, before we really get into this: How about this amazing production that you and your team have put together? This is truly incredible for its originality. These boxes that you were filming live, that's just crazy cool, so, thank you.

I think the great thing about humans in general is we're always improving things. And so if entrepreneurs and inventors follow their curiosity and they follow their passions, and they figure something out and they figure out how to make it better, and they're never satisfied. You need to harness that. In my view, you need to harness that energy primarily on your customers instead of on your competitors. I sometimes see companies, even young small startup companies or entrepreneurs go awry, is that they start to pay more attention to their competition than they do to their customers. I think that in big mature industries, that might be a winning approach in some cases they kind of close following. Let other people be the pioneers and go down the blind alleys. There are many things that a new, inventive company tries that won't work. Those mistakes and errors and failures do cost real money.

So maybe in a mature industry where growth rates are slow and change is very slow. But, as you see in the world more and more, there aren't that many mature industries. Change is happening everywhere. We see it in the automobile industry with self-driving cars, but you can go right down the line of every industry and see it.

Döpfner: But do you have any idea of where your ambition really comes from, what was driving you?

Bezos: I really don't know. I have been passionate about certain things forever, I fell in love with computers in fourth grade. I got very lucky, my elementary school had a teletype that was connected to a mainframe computer that some business in downtown Houston donated. You can picture these teletypes, they had the punch tape and a 300 baud modem. You would dial up the phone and put it in the cradle, we had some time-sharing on that mainframe computer, and none of the teachers knew how to use it, so me and two other kids stayed after school and sort of figured out how to do it, and kind of taught ourselves programming from books. I think one thing is, I got very lucky early in my childhood.

Look, we all get gifts, we get certain things in our life that we're very lucky about. One of the most powerful ones is who your early role models are, you know it could be . . .

Döpfner: Your grandfather.

Bezos: It was, in a big sense. My mom, my dad and my grandfather too. My mom had me when she was 17 years old, and she was still in high school, in Albuquerque, New Mexico, this is in 1964. I can assure you that being a pregnant teenager in high school was not cool in Albuquerque, New Mexico, at that time. It was very difficult for her, my grandfather went to bat for her, and then they tried to kick her out of school, they're incredible, so the gift I had was I that had this incredible family.

Döpfner: Could you describe a little bit the role of your grandfather? It seems he was particularly important to you.

Bezos: He was super important for me, I spent an unusual amount of time with my grandparents, and especially with my grandfather on the ranch. He had a ranch in South Texas, I would spend my summers there, from ages 4 to 16. When I was 4, they were taking me for the summer to kind of give my parents a break. I was so young, and it was useful. I was a handful, I'm sure. Anyway, he created the illusion for me when I was 4 years old that I was helping him on the ranch, which, of course, cannot have been true. But I believed it. By the time I was 16, of course, I was actually helping on the ranch. I could fix prolapsed cattle, we did all our own veterinary work. Some of the cattle even survived. We fixed windmills, laid water pipelines, built fences, barns, and fixed the bulldozer that you guys talked about. One of the things that's so interesting about that lifestyle and about my grandfather is he did everything himself. He didn't call a vet if one of the animals was sick, he figured out what to do himself.

Döpfner: So, the lesson was, if it really matters, there is no delegation?

Bezos: Being resourceful. If there's a problem, there's a solution. Of course as you get into the business world and anything you do in a team, you very quickly realize that it's not just about your own resourcefulness, it's about team resourcefulness and how that works. That attitude of my grandfather's, he was full of wisdom. And as John mentioned the story about the words my grandfather gave me at one point that "it's harder to be kind than clever."

That story, the slightly longer version of that story, because this is really powerful wisdom, is that I made my grandmother burst into tears. The way I did it was we were driving on a long road trip, and she was a chain-smoker. I was probably 10 years old, so this was around 1974, we were in a period of time where there were heavy anti-smoking radio advertisements trying to convince people to stop smoking. One of the advertisements had this figure in it that said something like, "Every puff of a cigarette takes so many minutes off your life." I think it was two minutes but can't remember.

So, I sat in the back of the car on this long car ride and calculated how many years she had taken off of her life. In my 10-year-old mind, I had been extremely clever to do this, and so when I was finished with my arithmetic, I proudly announced to her how many years she had taken off of her life. I got a reaction I did not expect, with her bursting into tears. So my grandfather stopped the car and he took me out of the car. I had no idea what was about to happen, because he had never said a cross word to me. I thought he might actually be angry with me. But he wasn't. He took me out so that we had some privacy from her and he said these incredible words. He said, "You're going to figure out one day that it's harder to be kind than clever."

Döpfner: Wonderful. And how about your brother? Is it true that he's still a firefighter?

Bezos: He is. He's a volunteer firefighter in Scarsdale, New York. He's also the funniest person I know. When I'm with him, I'm just laughing continuously. First of all, I'm a good audience, I mean, I laugh easily. But he is really very funny, and my sister too. We're all very close. I have my mother to thank for that because she worked hard to make sure as we grew up so that we stayed close together. She takes all the grandkids for one week every summer so that me and my sister and our spouses can go on a trip together. So we end up spending a lot of time together.

Döpfner: For me, the most moving image that we saw tonight was the one that John Elkann showed, where you and MacKenzie are constructing that famous office table. It is very moving because it shows how you really started from scratch, like two classmates. It illustrates, symbolically, that the launch of Amazon was really something that you did together. Could you describe a little bit what MacKenzie's role was?

Bezos: Well, first of all, MacKenzie had married this stable guy working on Wall Street, and a year after we got married, I went to her and said I wanted to quit my job, move across the country, and start this internet bookstore. MacKenzie, of course, like everybody I explained this to, her first question was: "What's the internet?" Because nobody knew. This was in 1994.

But even before she could say, "What's the internet?" she said, "Great, let's go!" Because she wanted to support it and she knew that I had always had this passion for invention and starting a company. I think, you know, MacKenzie is an example of this, what I was talking about with my mom and my dad, who's a Cuban immigrant, and came to the US when he was 16 in a refugee camp in the Everglades. They are so loving and supportive. When you have loving and supportive people in your life, like MacKenzie, my parents, my grandfather, my grandmother, you end up being able to take risks. Because I think it's one of those things, you kind of know that somebody's got your back. And so if you're thinking about it logically, it's an emotional thing.

Döpfner: Do you think if you feel and experience unconditional love, it helps you to take risks in life?

Bezos: I think it helps you. By the way, I think that's probably true for all kinds of risks in life, not just for starting a business. Life is full of different risks. I think that, when you think about the things that you will regret when you're 80, they're almost always the things that you did not do. They are acts of omission. Very rarely are you going to regret something that you did that failed and didn't work or whatever. But the acts of omission, again I'm not just talking about business things, it's, like, "I love that person and I never told them," and you know, 50 years later you're like, "Why didn't I tell her? Why didn't I go after it?" So that's the kind of life regret that is very hard to be happy about, when you're telling yourself in a private moment that story of your life. I've won that lottery of having so many people in my life who have given me that unconditional love, and I do think that MacKenzie's definitely one of those. So, we moved, and then MacKenzie, who basically has no skill in this area at all, did our accounting for the first year and she did it well, that's what's amazing.

My wife is a novelist, she won the American Book Award. Toni Morrison, the Nobel Prize-winning author, who was MacKenzie's teacher at Princeton, said on Charlie Rose show that MacKenzie was her best student ever. So MacKenzie is a very talented novelist, but she is not an accountant. But she pulled it off, and again, we all got done what we needed to get done.

Döpfner: Did she, being an author, suggest that you focus on the book business at the beginning?

Bezos: No, I picked books. It is true that she's a big reader and I'm a big reader. But that's not why I picked books. I picked books because there were more items in the book category than in any other category. And so you could build universal selection. There were 3 million in 1994 when I was pulling this idea together, 3 million different books active in print at any given time. The largest physical bookstores only had about 150,000 different titles. And so I could see how you could make a bookstore online with universal selection. Every book ever printed, even the out-of-print ones, was the original vision for the company. So that's why books.

Döpfner: When did you know that Amazon was going to be successful?

Bezos: Well, I knew that the books, strangely, I was very prepared for this to take a really long time, I knew that the books business was going to be successful in the first 30 days. I was shocked at how many books we sold. We were ill prepared. We had like, only 10 people in the company at that time. Most of them were software engineers, everybody including me and the software engineers were all packing boxes. We didn't even have packing tables. We were down on our hands and knees on a concrete floor, packing the boxes. At about 1 or 2 in the morning, I said to one of my software-engineering colleagues, I said, you know, Paul, this is killing my knees, we need to get knee pads. Paul looked at me and he was, like, Jeff, we need to get packing tables. And I was, like, oh my God, that is such a good idea. The next day I bought packing tables and it doubled our productivity, and probably saved our backs and knees too.

Döpfner: But Amazon had serious crises. You went almost bankrupt. What went wrong?

Bezos: We had so many. I haven't had any existential crises, knock on wood, I don't want to jinx anything. But we've had a lot of dramatic events. I remember early on, we only had 125 employees when Barnes & Noble, the big United States bookseller, opened their online website to compete against us, barnesandnoble.com. We'd had about a two-year window, we opened in 1995, they opened in 1997. At that time all of the headlines were on how we were about to be destroyed by this much larger company. We had 125 employees and $60 million a year in annual sales, $60 million with an "M." And

Barnes & Noble at that time had 30,000 employees and about $3 billion in sales. So they were giant; we were tiny. We had limited resources, and the headlines were very negative about Amazon. The one that was most memorable was just "Amazon.toast."

I called an all-hands meeting, which was not hard to do with just 125 people. We got in a room, and because it was so scary for all of us, this idea that now we finally had a big competitor. That literally everybody's parents were calling and saying, "Are you OK?" It's usually the moms calling and asking their children are you going to be OK? I said, "Look, it's OK to be afraid, but don't be afraid of our competitors, because they're never going to send us any money, be afraid of our customers. If we just stay focused on them, instead of obsessing over this big competitor that we just got, *we'll* be fine." I really do believe that. I think that if you stay focused the more drama there is and everything else, no matter what the drama is, whatever the actionable distraction is, your response to it should be to double down on the customer. Satisfy them. And not just satisfy them, delight them.

Döpfner: Amazon is employing 566,000 people. You're probably the biggest job creator of recent times. At the same time, you are aggressively criticized by unions and by the media for paying low wages for inappropriate working conditions. How do you deal with these accusations?

Bezos: Well, first of all, with any criticism, my approach to criticism and what I teach and preach inside Amazon, is when you're criticized, first look in a mirror and decide, are your critics right? If they're right, change. Don't resist.

Döpfner: Are they right?

Bezos: No. Not in this case. But we've had critics be right before, and we changed. We have made mistakes, I can go through a long list. One of the early most painful ones is so stupid, it's hard to believe how we ever did it. But early on with the Kindle, either the first year of the Kindle or the second year, we had accidentally illegally sold, or given away I guess, copies of the famous novel "1984." Because it had a complicated copyright history, it was in copyright in the US and not in the UK, or something strange like this, so it was in the public domain, but only in certain geographies. And we had screwed that up somehow. This is the kind of mistake that only a corporation can make, an individual can't make this mistake because somehow it happens at the intersections of the different teams, so you've got the legal department saying, "Oh crap, we've made this mistake" and you've got the book's team. And anyway, the answer the company came up with was to, and we did this without warning, just electronically go into everybody's Kindle who had downloaded that book and just disappear it. So, it was as if we'd walked into your bedroom in the middle of the night, found your bookshelf, and just took that book away. We were rightly criticized for that, and we responded to that.

On the issue of working conditions, I'm very proud of our working conditions and very proud of the wages we pay. You know, in Germany we employ 16,000 people and we pay at the high end of the range for any comparable work.

Döpfner: So, is it a union fight, because the union wants to make sure you are unionized, or what is the real substance of the conflict?

Bezos: It's a good question. And this is in my longer version of how to deal with critics.

There are two kinds of critics. There are well-meaning critics who are worried it's not going to work, but they do want it to work. I can give you an example, customer reviews would be one of those. When we first did customer reviews 20 years ago, some book publishers were not happy about it because some of them were negative, so it was a very controversial practice at that time, but we thought it was right and so we stuck to our guns and had a deep keel on that and it didn't change. But there's a second kind of critic, which is the self-interested critic, and they come in all shapes and sizes. They can be any kind of institution, competitors, of course. When you are doing something in a new way and if customers embrace the new way, what's going to happen is incumbents who are practicing the older way are not going to like you. And they're going to be self-interested critics.

And so you do need, as you're looking at yourself in the mirror, to try and tease those two things apart. In our view, we have workers' councils, of course, and we have very good communications with our employees. We don't believe that we need a union to be an intermediary between us and our employees but, of course, at the end of the day, it's always the employees' choice. And that's how it should be. But for sure we would be very naïve to believe that we're not going to be criticized, that's just part of the terrain, you have to accept that. One thing that I tell people is if you're going to do anything new or innovative, you have to be willing to be misunderstood. If you cannot afford to be misunderstood, then for goodness' sake, don't do anything new or innovative.

Döpfner: Maggie Thatcher said, "Leadership is not to be pleased by the moment."

Bezos: Perfect.

Döpfner: But your most prominent critic at the moment is the president of the United States. People are even saying that he may be willing to prepare initiatives to break up Amazon, because it's too big, it's too successful, it's too dominant in too many sectors, or for varied other reasons, including the fact that he doesn't like The Post. Is this break-up scenario something that you take seriously, or do you think it's just a fantasy?

Bezos: For me, again, this is one of those things where I focus on, and ask our teams to focus on what we can control, and I expect, whether it's the current US administration or any other government agency around the world, Amazon is now a large corporation and I expect us to be scrutinized. We should be scrutinized. I think all large institutions should be scrutinized and examined. It's reasonable. One thing to note about is that we have gotten big in absolute terms only very recently. So we've always been growing very fast in percentage terms, but in 2010, just eight years ago, we had 30,000 employees. So in the last eight years we've gone from 30,000 employees to 560,000 employees.

You know, in my mind, I'm still delivering the packages to the post office myself. You see what I'm saying? I still have all the memories of hoping that one day we could afford a forklift. So obviously my intellectual brain knows that's just not the case anymore. We have 560,000 employees all over the world. And I know we should be scrutinized and I think it's true that big government institutions should be scrutinized, big nonprofit institutions should be scrutinized, big universities should be scrutinized. It just makes sense. And that's, by the way, why the work at The Washington Post and all other great newspapers around the world do, is so important. They are often the ones doing that initiate scrutiny, even before the government agencies do.

Döpfner: The general sentiment concerning the big innovative tech companies has changed. Facebook, Google, Amazon, Apple: They used to be seen as the nice guys in T-shirts who are saving the world. Now they are sometimes portrayed as the evil of the world. The debate about the Big 4 or the Big 5 is heating up: Professors like Scott Galloway and The Economist are suggesting a split-up, other powerful people like George Soros are giving very critical speeches at Davos, and the EU Commission is taking pretty tough positions here. Do you think that there is a change in the mindset of society, and how should the big tech companies, how should Amazon deal with that?

Bezos: I think it's a natural instinct. I think we humans, especially in the Western world, and especially inside democracies, are wired to be skeptical and mindful of large institutions of any kind. We're skeptical always of our government in the United States, state governments, and local governments. I assume it's similar in Germany. It's healthy, because they're big, powerful institutions, the police, the military, or whatever it is. It doesn't mean you don't trust them, or that they're bad or evil or anything like that. It's just that they have a lot of power and control, and so you want to inspect them. Maybe that's a better word, you kind of want to always be inspecting them. And if you look at the big tech companies, they have gotten large enough that they need and are going to be inspected. And by the way, it's not personal. I think you can go astray on this if you're the founder of a company, one of these big tech companies, or any other big institution. If you go astray on this, you might start to take it personally. Like, "Why are you someone inspecting me?" And I wish that people would just say, "Yes, it's fine."

Döpfner: The whole attitude toward data protection and privacy has always been different between Europe and the United States, but it is also at the moment, in the context of events like Cambridge Analytica, changing in the United States. Is this criticism hysterical or is it appropriate? And what are the consequences for a company like Amazon?

Bezos: I think this is one of the great questions of our age. I think of the internet like this big, new, powerful technology. It's horizontal. It affects every industry. And if you think of it even more broadly, it's tech and machine learning, big data, and all these kinds of things. These are big, horizontal, powerful technologies. And in my view the internet is quite old at this point; we've been around a long time. But that scale has only been around 10 or 15 years. You know, go back in time 20 years and it was tiny. And so that scale has only been around 10 or 15 years. And so we haven't learned as a civilization and a human species how to operate that yet. We as a civilization are still figuring all of that out. It gives us fantastic capabilities. The fact that I can look up almost anything on Wikipedia in five seconds is an unbelievable capability that just simply didn't exist 20 years ago. And so on and so on. But we're also finding out that these powerful tools enable some very bad things, too, like letting authoritarian governments interfere in free democratic elections in the world. This is an incredibly scary thing.

Döpfner: So you are advocating a balance of, say, entrepreneurs who are really moving their businesses forward, politicians and regulators who are defining a certain framework, society and journalists who are asking unpleasant questions?

Bezos: My view on Amazon's role in this, which is what you asked me. I think, first of all, we have a duty on behalf of society to try and help educate any regulators, to give them our point of view sincerely, without any cynicism or skepticism. This is what we believe. But it's not ultimately our decision, so we will work with any set of regulations that were given. Ultimately, society decides that. We will follow those rules regardless of the impact they have on our business. And we will find a new way, if need be, to delight customers.

What you have to worry about and the problem I would not want to see happen is that you don't want to block innovation and invention. One of the unintended consequences often of regulation is that it really favors the incumbents. Now, Amazon at this point is an incumbent, so maybe I should be happy about that. But I wouldn't be because I think for society, you really want to see continued progress. To the degree that we have regulation, we want to be sure that it is incenting innovation and not blocking it, while at the same time, regarding data security, privacy, encryption, how do you safeguard people's physical safety against terrorists and bad actors all over the world, and how do you balance that against privacy? These are very challenging questions. And we're not going to answer them, even in a few years. I think it's going to be an ongoing thing for quite a while.

Döpfner: Data security and privacy are going to be competitive advantages for companies, or a disadvantage for those who are not dealing respectfully and responsibly with data?

Bezos: I 100% agree with this. One of the reasons we have been able to extend into new business areas and pursue new product categories. Going way back, we just sold books, then we started selling music and DVDs, electronics, toys and so on, then we extended into electronic reading with Kindle. The reason customers have been receptive in large part to our new initiatives is because we have worked hard to earn their trust. Earning trust with customers is a valuable business asset. If you mistreat their data, they will know, they will figure it out. Customers are very smart, you should never underestimate customers.

Döpfner: You're preparing a second headquarters. It's going to be in the US. Why didn't you consider doing it in Europe?

Bezos: I wanted it in a time zone either in Canada, the US, or Mexico.

Döpfner: So it's not an anti-Europe decision?

Bezos: No, absolutely not.

Döpfner: When you bought The Post there were people saying, "Well, that's just a personal toy, he wants to have some political influence in Washington." Other people thought it was a new long-term element of your strategy. So what was it?

Bezos: You can explain things to people, but you can't understand things to people. All I can do is say really what my thought process was. I was not looking to buy a newspaper. It had never even crossed my mind. So when the opportunity came up, because I had known Don Graham at that point for 15 years. And any of you who are lucky enough to know Don knows that he is the most honorable gentleman that you'll ever meet. You know him very well. He's a remarkable guy. He so loved The Post that he believed, even if this was a huge personal sacrifice for him because it had been in his family for so long, that he needed to find a new home for it.

I think there were certain purchasers he was hoping would not end up buying The Post, because he wanted it to remain independent. So when he approached me with this I said, "You know, I'm the wrong guy, because I don't know anything about the newspaper business." He said, "That's OK, because we have a lot of people at The Post who know a lot about the newspaper business. What we really need is somebody who knows something more about the internet. The Post was in a very difficult financial position at that time. So for me I had to decide, "Was it hopeless?" I didn't believe it was hopeless. I was optimistic that The Post could turn around. And then, second, I had to decide, "Did I want to put my own time and energy into this?" That, for me, I just had to ask the simple question: "Is it an important institution?" The answer to that question is yes. It was very obvious to me as soon as I thought about it that way, it was like OK, I think I actually can help in two ways. I can provide financial resources while this turn around occurs. I can also help with my internet knowledge. Is it an institution worth saving? You bet! It's the most important newspaper in the most important capital city in the Western world. I'd be crazy not to save that newspaper. I'm going to be very happy when I'm 80 that I made that decision.

Döpfner: Have you seen Steven Spielberg's film "The Post"? And how did you like it?

Bezos: I have, I've seen it a couple of times.

Döpfner: What's the lesson that you learned from that, and could you imagine also to buy other newspapers?

Bezos: No, I get that request monthly. I really do. I tell them, no. The Post is it for me. I'm not interested in buying other newspapers. I watched that movie, and it's helpful. I loved that movie, and also reading Katherine Graham's memoir, which won a Pulitzer Prize and is an amazing book. Because it gets me ready. You know, as the owner of The Post, I know that at times The Post is going to write stories that are going to make very powerful people very unhappy.

Döpfner: Are you upset if the Post journalists are writing critical stories about Amazon?

Bezos: No, I'm not upset at all.

Döpfner: Did or would you ever interfere?

Bezos: Never. I would be humiliated to interfere. I would be so embarrassed. I would turn bright red. I just don't want to, it would feel icky, it would feel gross. It would be one of those things when I'm 80 years old I would be so unhappy with myself if I had interfered. Why would I? I want that paper to be independent. We have a fantastic editor in Marty Baron. We have a fantastic publisher in Fred Ryan. The head of our technology team, a guy named Shailesh, is fantastic. They don't need my help in the newsroom for sure. First of all, that's also an expert's job. It would be like me getting on the airplane and going up to the front of the plane and saying to the pilot, "You should move aside, let me do this!"

Döpfner: Well, you are not flying airplanes, but you are sending rockets to the orbit. Could you share with us the vision of Blue Origin and the idea of space tourism with reusable rockets?

Bezos: Yes. This is super important to me, and I believe on the longest timeframe, and really here I'm thinking of a timeframe of a couple of hundred years, so over millions of decades, I believe and I get increasing conviction with every passing year, that Blue Origin, the space company, is the most important work that I'm doing. And so there is a whole plan for Blue Origin.

Döpfner: Really, so you'd say retail, e-commerce, clouds, publishing, that's all less relevant than the space project?

Bezos: Yes, and I'll tell you why.

First of all, of course, I'm interested in space, because I'm passionate about it. I've been studying it and thinking about it since I was a 5-year-old boy. But that is not why I'm pursuing this work. I'm pursuing this work, because I believe if we don't, we will eventually end up with a civilization of stasis, which I find very demoralizing. I don't want my great-grandchildren's great-grandchildren to live in a civilization of stasis. We all enjoy a dynamic civilization of growth and change. Let's think about what powers that. We are not really energy-constrained.

Let me give you just a couple of numbers. If you take your body, your metabolic rate as a human, it's just an animal. You eat food, that's your metabolism. You burn about 100 watts. Your power, your body, is the same as a 100-watt lightbulb. We're incredibly efficient. Your brain is about 60 watts of that. Amazing. But if you extrapolate in developed countries where we use a lot of energy, on average in developed countries our civilizational metabolic rate is 11 000 watts. So, in a natural state, where we're animals, we're only using 100 watts. In our actual developed-world state, we're using 11,000 watts. And it's growing. For a century or more, it's been compounding at a few percent a year, our energy usage as a civilization.

Now if you take baseline energy usage globally across the whole world and compound it at just a few percent a year for just a few hundred years, you have to cover the entire surface of the Earth in solar cells. That's the real energy crisis. And it's happening soon. And by soon, I mean within just a few 100 years. We don't actually have that much time. So what can you do? Well, you can have a life of stasis, where you cap how much energy we get to use. You have to work only on efficiency. By the way, we've always been working on energy efficiency, and still we grow our energy usage. It's not like we have been squandering energy. We have been getting better at using it with every passing decade. So, stasis would be very bad, I think.

Now take the scenario, where you move out into the solar system. The solar system can easily support a trillion humans. And if we had a trillion humans, we would have a thousand

Einsteins and a thousand Mozarts, and unlimited for all practical purposes, resources and solar power. That's the world that I want my great-grandchildren's great-grandchildren to live in.

By the way, I believe that in that timeframe we will move all heavy industry off of Earth and Earth will be zoned residential and light industry. It will basically be a very beautiful planet. We have sent robotic probes to every planet in this solar system now and believe me this is the best one.

Döpfner: Jeff, when can I buy the first ticket to do a little space tour?

BezoSo the first tourism vehicle, we won't be selling tickets yet, but we may put humans in it at the end of this year or at the beginning of next year. We are very close. We are building a very large orbital vehicle. We have been working on that for more than five years. It will fly for the first time in 2020. The key is reusability. This civilization I'm talking about of getting comfortable living and working in space and having millions of people and then billions of people and then finally a trillion people in space. You can't do that with space vehicles that you use once and then throw away. It's a ridiculous, costly way to get into space.

Döpfner: The most recent thing you are planning seems to be home robots. I assume it is more than Alexa walking. What is the vision behind it?

Bezos: I saw that rumor in the press, and I can't comment on that.

Döpfner: So I see it seems to be very serious. Jeff, you are one of the most long-term-thinking entrepreneurs when it comes to companies, products, and services. If it is about philanthropy, you recently said that you are a very short-term thinker. You really want to deal with the now and here. I think that is also very innovative. Can you explain that approach?

Bezos: I am going to end up doing a mixture of things. We started doing in Seattle, there is a homeless shelter called Mary's Place, run by a woman named Marty. That has really impacted my thinking on this issue, because what I'm seeing is, I'm in favor of all, long-term-oriented philanthropy is also very good idea. I'm not against that. I'm finding I am very motivated by the here and now. Seeing a lot of the homelessness that Mary's Place works on is transient homelessness. When you go study homelessness, there are a bunch of causes of homelessness. Mental-incapacity issues are a very hard-to-cure problem. Serious drug addictions are very hard-to-cure problems. But there is another bucket of homelessness, it is this transient homelessness. Which is, you know, a woman with kids, the father runs away and he was the only person providing any income. They have no support system; they have no family, that's transient homelessness. You can really help that person, and by the way, you only have to help them for six to nine months. You get them trained. You get them a job. They are perfectly productive members of society.

Döpfner: Last week we had Bill Gates for dinner here and he said in a self-ironic manner that he has a ridiculous amount of money and it is so hard to find appropriate ways to spend that money reasonably and to do good with the money. So what does money mean to you, being the first person in history who has a net worth of a three-digit amount of billions.

Bezos: The only way that I can see to deploy this much financial resource is by converting my Amazon winnings into space travel. That is basically it. Blue Origin is expensive enough to be able to use that fortune. I am liquidating about $1 billion a year of Amazon stock to fund Blue Origin. I plan to continue to do that for a long time. Because you're right, you're not going to spend it on a second dinner out. That's not what we are talking about. I am very lucky that I feel like I have a mission-driven purpose with Blue Origin that is, I think, incredibly important for civilization long term. I am going to use my financial lottery winnings from Amazon to fund that.

Döpfner: With regard to your personal lifestyle, there are no guilty pleasures, unreasonable things that you do with money?

Bezos: I don't think they're that guilty. I mean, I have lots of pleasures, and we just came back from an amazing trip with the kids, MacKenzie and I did. She planned the whole thing. It was her birthday trip, but she planned it all. We went to Norway for three days and we stayed in an ice hotel. We went dogsledding, we went to a wolf preserve and actually got to interact with timber wolves. It really was an incredible vacation, a pretty incredible holiday. We got it all done in three and a half days. It was amazing.

Döpfner: You are a family man. Your kids are extremely important for you. You seem to be the ideal father. If we were to talk to your kids, what would they criticize about their dad?

Bezos: They would make fun of my singing. They would make fun of my inability to remember exact words. I am always quoting Churchill or something and am getting it wrong. And they're, like, "That's not even close to what Churchill said!" They would probably, depending on the moment, they might criticize my laugh. They're kids! I am lucky. I have very good relationship with them. This work-life harmony thing is what I try to teach young employees and actually senior executives at Amazon too. But especially the people coming in. I get asked about work-life balance all the time. And my view is, that's a debilitating phrase because it implies there's a strict trade-off. The reality is, if I am happy at home, I come into the office with tremendous energy. If I am happy at work, I come home with tremendous energy. It actually is a circle; it's not a balance. I think that is worth everybody paying attention to it. You never want to be that guy, and we all have a coworker who's that person, who as soon as they come into a meeting they drain all the energy out of the room. You can just feel the energy go *whoosh!* You don't want to be that guy. You want to come into the office and give everyone a kick in their step.

Döpfner: Jeff, thank you very much. We congratulate you for all you have achieved.

Jeff Bezos and Brother Mark Bezos Fireside Talk

(2017)

Mark Bezos: This gentleman certainly needs no introduction. My name is Mark Bezos and you're all welcome to call me what my friends do, they usually just refer to me as Jeff's brother.

Jeff Bezos: By the way, just so you know it actually does go both ways. My brother has a TED talk about small acts of kindness, being a volunteer firefighter and it has millions of views. Every once in a while, somebody will stop me and say, I love your TED talk about being a firefighter and small acts of kindness. I usually say well, thank you, but that's really my brother, his TED talk. But if I'm in a hurry, I just say thank you.

Mark Bezos: Yes, absolutely. But if any of you do get confused, I'm the one with the smaller bank account to your left.

Jeff Bezos: He's the big brother.

Mark Bezos: Jeff, before we get started, I think this is obviously a crowd of influential people. People who are starting out, I think we might as well just make the most of their time. I'm just going to dive right into this, if you don't mind.

Jeff Bezos: Let's go.

Mark Bezos: So you are captain of industry, Amazon.com, private space flight with Blue Origin, The Washington Post, levels of fame and wealth that are hard to comprehend. I guess one question that probably is at the top of everyone's mind is, if you had to choose one thing, what would you say is your favorite part of having me as a little brother? Because I've taken the liberty of writing down some thoughts.

Jeff Bezos: I know the answer to this. There are many things I love about having Mark as a brother, but what, he just did is number one at the top of the list. When I am with my brother, I just laugh continuously.

Mark Bezos: Yes.

Jeff Bezos: Because he is the funniest guy in my life.

Mark Bezos: Well, thank you. You're an easy audience and I appreciate it so.

Jeff Bezos: I am actually an easy audience. That is true.

Mark Bezos: All right. So, here's what we're going to do if all of you don't mind. The fact that a fireside chat among brothers, this is not unique for us. This is something that we do quite often, it's rare that we have a couple thousand of our closest friends with us.

Jeff Bezos: We go through in front of an audience, and we usually actually have a fire.

Mark Bezos: Yes and bourbon. So, what we're going to talk about, the things that I'm going to chat with Jeff about are not, the sorts of things perhaps that you would hear in most interviews. Because two pizza rules is not really my jam, so we're not going to talk about those things. But we do have a shared history, so, what I really want to focus on is the influences and the inspirations that have led to some of the things.

Jeff Bezos: This is a little intimidating, he knows way too much.

Mark Bezos: What I'd like to do is invite all of you to join in on what is I believe are some of our greatest hits I guess, from my point of view. Because we have such a shared history, what I've done, much to Jeff's chagrin is I've gone through and taken the liberty of pulling together a bunch of family photos. I'm going to be throwing some of those up behind us and just so that you guys can sort of understand. If we start talking shorthand, you'll understand what it is that we're referring to. All sound good? All right. I am going to, and I appreciate your patience, this is not the sort of thing that I usually do, so I appreciate your patience. We're just going to dive right into it. When we were kids, we would spend every summer on our grandfather's ranch in South Texas.

Jeff Bezos: We were probably just fixing that windmill.

Mark Bezos: Yes. Always fixing windmills.

Mark Bezos: Before you were climbing them and smashing bottles upon them, which you did recently in an Instagram video. So, one of the things that we would do every summer, it was really a magical experience. There's little Jeff.

Jeff Bezos: Yes. That was my maximum cuteness right there. So, by the way, all downhill from there. That's a 1962

International Harvester Scout, we all learned to drive in that car. Once you can drive that car, you can drive anything.

Mark Bezos: There's the two of us, that is Jeff teaching me how to open or close a gate, which doesn't seem like it would be that complicated, but I was having trouble.

Jeff Bezos: Wire gap gates are tough.

Mark Bezos: I guess one of the things that we learned every summer is to value, and you've spoken about this in the past, is the role that resourcefulness, self-reliance plays.

Jeff Bezos: Yes, for sure.

Mark Bezos: Can you talk a little bit about it?

Jeff Bezos: Well, first of all, we had a very fortunate, lucky childhood. We got to spend a lot of time with pop and our grandparents, and you learn different things from grandparents, and you learn from parents, it's just a very different relationship. I spent all my summers on his ranch from age 4 to 16 and, he was incredibly self-reliant. You know if you're in the middle of nowhere in a rural area, you don't pick up the phone and call somebody when something breaks, you figure out how to fix it yourself. So as a kid, I got to see him solve all these problems and be a real problem solver. Even did his own veterinary work, he would make his own needles to suture up the cattle with. He would like take a piece of wire, use a blow torch to heat it up, pound it flat, sharpen it, drill a hole through it, make a needle. Some of the cattle even survived and so we learned a lot of things from watching him. Because he would take on major projects that he didn't really know how to do, and then figure out how to do them.

Mark Bezos: A good example of that is you guys built a house.

Jeff Bezos: Yes, I think he bought this out of a Sears catalog. It was a kit house, and we built that thing. It all showed up in big boxes and somebody, a professional came out and poured the foundation and then we did the rest of it. But yes that was quite a project. I think that if you can talk a little bit, I know that there is this bulldozer in the background.

Yes, that's a D6 Caterpillar bulldozer that my grandfather bought used for $5,000, which was an enormous bargain, you know it should cost way more than that. The reason it was so cheap was because it was completely broken. The transmission was stripped, the hydraulics didn't work. We spent basically a whole summer repairing it, big giant gears would arrive by mail order from Caterpillar. We couldn't even move the gears, so the first thing my grandfather did was build a crane to move the gear. That's the kind of self-reliance and resourcefulness.

Mark Bezos: There's also a story that is somewhat legendary in our family, one of the things that Pop did one summer. It was a little out of character.

Jeff Bezos: Oh, I know what story you're talking about. He really actually was a very careful, conservative sort of person. Not prone to crazy acts or anything, he was kind of introspective and very introverted, quiet person. One day he was all by himself, he had driven to the ranch, he was at the main gate to the ranch and he forgot to put the car in park. When he got to the gate, he noticed that the car was slowly rolling downhill toward the gate. He thought this is fantastic, I have just enough time to unlatch the gate, throw the gate open. The car's going to drive right through and that will be wonderful. He almost got the gate unlatched when the car hit the gate, it caught his thumb between the gate and the fence post and it stripped all the flesh off of his thumb. It was hanging there by a tiny little thread, he was so angry at himself that he ripped that piece of flesh off and threw it in the brush. Got back in the car, drove himself to the emergency room in Dilley, Texas 16 miles away. When he got there, they said this is great, we can reattach that, where is it? He said, I threw it in the brush. They drove back with the nurses and everybody, and they looked for hours for the thumb, and they never found that piece of flesh, something probably eaten it.

They took him back to the emergency room and they said look, you have two choices. You're going to have a skin graft for that, and we can sew your thumb to your stomach and leave it there for six weeks. That's the best way to do it or we can just cut a piece of skin graft from your butt and just suture it on, and it won't ever be as good, but the advantage is your thumb won't be sewn to your stomach for six weeks. He said, I'll take option 2, just do the skin graft from my butt. They did that, it was very successful, it worked fine. I have incredibly vivid memories, how his mornings were completely ritualized.

He'd wake up, eat breakfast cereal, read the newspaper and shave with an electric razor for a really long time. Like he would shave with that electric razor for like 15 minutes, while he's eating his cereal. When he was done shaving his face with that razor, then he would take two quick passes over his thumb because his thumb grew butt hair. Which by the way, did not bother him at all.

Mark Bezos: No, he was completely unfazed by it,

Jeff Bezos: Yes unfazed.

Mark Bezos: So, thumb butt hair side, the value of resourcefulness.

Jeff Bezos: Yes.

Mark Bezos: Right and self-reliance. How do you apply that to the work that you do on a daily basis?

Jeff Bezos: Well, I think and there are a lot of entrepreneurs and people pursuing dreams and passions. The whole point of moving things forward is if you run into problems, run into failures, things don't work, you have to back up and try again. Each one of those times when you have a setback, you back up and you try again. You're using resourcefulness, you're using self-reliance, you're trying to invent your way out of a box. We have tons of examples at Amazon where we've had to do this. We failed so many times, I always think of us as a great place to fail because we're good at it, we have so much practice. I get just to give you one example, many years ago now, we wanted a third party selling business because we knew we could add selection to the store that way. We started Amazon Auctions, nobody came. I think maybe our mother is the only one who purchased something.

Mark Bezos: I bought a coffee cup.

Jeff Bezos: Okay. So, there were two purchasers and then we said, well, what can we do? We opened this thing called Z shops, which was like fixed price auctions, again, nobody came.

Mark Bezos: I didn't use that.

Jeff Bezos: Then finally, each one of these failures is like a year, year and a half long. So, we're trying to invent new things and we finally came across this idea of putting the third-party selection on the same detailed pages. The same product detail pages that we had our own retail inventory on. We called this marketplace, and it started working right away. That is resourcefulness of trying new things, figuring things out and what the customers really want.

It pays off in everything and it pays off even in your daily lives. How do you help your children, what's the right thing? My wife has a great saying, we let our kids use, now they're 17 through 12, even when they were 4, we would let them use sharp knives and by the time they were, maybe 7 or 8, we'd let them use certain power tools. My wife much to her credit, has this great saying, she said I would much rather have a kid with nine fingers than a resourceless kid, which I just think is a fantastic attitude about life.

Mark Bezos: It was a prerequisite for the selection of a spouse, right?

Jeff Bezos: Yes, in my twenties, this is way pre-Tinder, pre-Match.com. I decided I wanted to get married, I had all my friends set me up and I had my list of criteria, and this was like good, old-fashioned blind dates. I went on dozens of them, and it turned out I kept meeting people who were professional blind daters and I sort of became a professional blind dater. We would sit down and most of the conversation was quickly about how we're not right for each other, but how do you meet people? When I was telling my friends my criteria, one that I would list was that I wanted a woman who could get me out of a third world prison. My friends were like what are your future plans? I said, no, it's just a visualization for somebody really resourceful, because I think that if you don't want to go through life with teammates who aren't resourceful, you do want to go through life with people who can get you out of a third world prison.

Mark Bezos: Hypothetically speaking.

Jeff Bezos: Hypothetically speaking.

Mark Bezos: Your eating habits at this point in your life were not great.

Jeff Bezos: No. You won't even believe this story; you just have to believe me that what I tell you is true. When my wife and I got married, for a couple of years I had been eating for breakfast every morning a whole can of Pillsbury biscuits. I would wake up in the morning, preheat the oven to 375, I would get out the baking sheet, crack open the Pillsbury biscuit lay some there with butter and I would eat the whole can. I was skinny as real. After we got married, she watched me do this every morning for like three months. Then she finally stopped me one day and said, do you know what's in that? I was like, honestly that wasn't even a concept for me that there was something in food. I had never read a nutrition label in my life, I ate what tasted good to me. She kind of showed me the ingredients label, we had a little, very rudimentary discussion about nutrition and I stopped eating the biscuits.

Mark Bezos: One of the things I want to talk about, a question that we've talked about before. You were 30 years old in 1994. When you decided to start Amazon.com, you had a great job, I remember you had a great apartment on the Upper West Side.

Jeff Bezos: Been married for a year. I had not been eating biscuits for nine months.

Mark Bezos: How did you go through making the decision to drop what was a very good job and take this chance? It all seems very obvious now, right, this many years later that it paid off, but at the time it was not obvious.

Jeff Bezos: No, no, it wasn't. I did do a lot of soul-searching, I went to my boss at the time, and I really liked my job. I told him I was going to go do this thing, start an internet bookstore. I'd already told my wife and she's like, great let's go! he said this is a good idea, but it would be an even better idea for somebody who didn't already have a good job. That sort of made some logical sense to me and he convinced me to think about it for a couple of days. I went away and was really trying to get my head around how to think about this.

I think for me the right way to make that kind of very personal decision, because those decisions are personal, they're not like data-driven business decisions, is what does your heart say? For me, the best way to think about it was to project myself forward to age 80 and say look when I'm 80 years old, I want to have minimized the number of regrets that I have. I don't want to be 80 years old in a quiet moment of reflection, thinking back over my life and cataloged a bunch of major regrets. I think that regrets, our biggest regrets in most cases, can murder somebody. In most cases, our biggest regrets turn out to be acts of omission, paths not taken, and they haunt us.

We wonder what would happen. I loved that person and I never told them, and then they married somebody else. That's the frame of mind that I put myself in. Once I did that, once I thought about it that way, it was immediately obvious to me. I knew that when I'm 80, I would never regret trying this thing that I was super excited about and failing. If it failed fine, I would be very proud of the fact when I'm 80, that I tried. I also knew that it would always haunt me if I didn't try. That would be a regret, it would be a hundred percent chance of a regret if I didn't try and basically a 0% chance of regret if I tried and failed. I think that's a useful metric for any important life decision.

Mark Bezos: A question I have is, we just talked about the fact that there was certainly no guarantee that Amazon was going to work.

Jeff Bezos: No, there never are, in any kind of startup.

Mark Bezos: What would Jeff Bezos be doing if this hadn't worked out?

Jeff Bezos: It's a good question. Nobody ever really knows what twists and turns life takes. My best guess is I would be a very happy software engineer.

Mark Bezos: Working on anything in particular?

Jeff Bezos: Well today, I'm very, very curious about machine learning and artificial intelligence and at Amazon we're doing a lot of that. Probably I would be attracted to that.

Mark Bezos: I thought of this question, not sure exactly how you would answer it, but I am curious to know your fantasy job, not the one that would pay the bills.

Jeff Bezos: Well that I have, and you know what it is.

Mark Bezos: My guess is, bartender.

Jeff Bezos: I pride myself on my craft cocktails and I do have this fantasy that I want to be a bartender. I know that it is a fantasy like if I were actually a bartender. I've glamorized the job in my mind I know that. But I love people, I like talking to people. I love making cocktails.

Mark Bezos: You're not very fast.

Jeff Bezos: I'm super slow. It would have to be a craft cocktail bar, we'd have to charge a lot per drink, and there'd be a big sign behind the bar that says you can have it good, or you can have it fast, which one do you want? But yes, I have a kind of fantasy there.

Mark Bezos: If we could shift the gears a little bit, I want to talk about Blue Origin. So Blue Origin is your private space flight, commercial space flight. We'll talk in a minute about all the work that you're doing in that regard. But I guess what I want to focus on for a minute or two is the inspiration for that. The passion behind it.

So, you were the valedictorian of your high school in Miami, and had the opportunity to give a speech at your graduation, I think the vast majority of your speech was about colonizing space.

Jeff Bezos: I think all of it.

Mark Bezos: Right. I still remember your closing line. I mean even then, it stood out to me. Do you remember it?

Jeff Bezos: I do remember, it was something like space, the final frontier, meet me there.

Mark Bezos: That was it.

Jeff Bezos: Yes. I've been passionate about space rockets and rocket engines since I was a five-year-old boy.

Mark Bezos: I want to talk about that a little bit, or certainly the story you've told about having seen the moon landing in 1969, right? Do you remember watching the lunar landing?

Jeff Bezos: Yes, and I do think you never know exactly, you don't choose your passions, your passions choose you. How they're formed you're never completely sure, but I do think you get imprinted somehow early on with certain things. You just get excited about them and because you're excited, you pay more attention, and they grow. Space is like that for me, I watched Neil Armstrong step onto the moon when I was five.

Mark Bezos: I do wonder, I know that Pop was a big fan of the Watergate trials.

Jeff Bezos: He was kind of a news junkie anyway. He obsessively watched the Watergate hearings.

Mark Bezos: Do you think at some level that might've influenced you?

Jeff Bezos: At least to buy the Post?

Mark Bezos: Yes, just curious.

Jeff Bezos: It's hard to know. You know I bought the Post because I think it's an important institution. I told the team at the time, the Post was kind of financially upside down, had a lot of work to do. No fault of their own, the internet had really taken the wind out of newspaper companies. I said look, I would not buy a financially upside-down salty snack food company, but The Post is a real institution and needs some runway. So that's why I did it.

I happened to know the guy who had owned it for so many years. Don Graham, who's just an amazing person, and so that all worked out. But did watching the Watergate hearings with Pop on the carpet have influenced that? Probably.

Mark Bezos: Going back to Blue Origin, I mean space has been such a big part of your life for so long and certainly every memory.

I think the science fiction movies, books, you know my passion for that stuff certainly came from watching you enjoy it so much.

If you could just take a minute or two and sort of help us understand what is Blue Origin up to?

Jeff Bezos: Well, the vision for Blue Origin is millions of people living and working in space. The key thing is we have to dramatically reduce the cost of access to space. Right now space travel is very expensive and the reason it's expensive, it's not hard to understand, is because we throw the hardware away after each use. So, we need reusable rocket vehicles, and that's what Blue Origin is working on. We're working on making sure that we don't have to throw the plane away every time after you fly out to your vacation destination. That would definitely increase the cost of your vacation. So that's what we need to do, and we can do it, it's totally possible and I think it's important.

My view is that it's incredibly important work that needs to be done and done as quickly as possible. I have my own reasons why I believe that they can be explained pretty simply. There's a very kind of common argument that's been routed for a long time, actually kind of first popularized by Arthur C. Clarke, who said all civilizations will become spacefaring or extinct. This is the kind of plan B argument that when earth is destroyed somehow we better make sure that we don't have all of our eggs in one basket. I hate the plan B argument. I think plan B with respect to earth being destroyed is making sure plan A works. So we have sent robotic probes to every planet in this solar system.

Believe me, this is the best one. We know that it's not even close. My friends who say they want to move to Mars or something, I say why don't you go live in Antarctica for a year first, because it's a garden paradise compared to Mars. Really, this planet is so amazing, it's a jewel in our solar system. If you take baseline energy usage and just compounded at a few percent a year for just a few hundred years, you have to cover the entire earth's surface in solar cells. So that's not going to happen, we have two choices: we either go out into space or we switch over to a civilization of stasis. Personally, I do not like the idea of stasis.

Our grandchildren and their grandchildren will live in a much better world if they can continue to advance and develop and use more energy and all of the things that we've enjoyed for hundreds of years as a civilization of growth. I don't even really believe in stasis, I think things are either growing or shrinking. I think stasis is highly unusual and in real life doesn't exist. I don't even think liberty is consistent with the idea of stasis. I mean if you get real stasis, somebody is going to have to tell you how many kids you can have, how much energy you can use. There'll be all kinds of things that just aren't consistent with Liberty and freedom. In space we have for all practical purposes, unlimited resources. We can have a trillion humans in the solar system and it still wouldn't be crowded. So then if you had a trillion humans, you'd have 1,000 Einsteins and a thousand Mozart and a thousand Da Vinci and how cool would that be?

But we have to go to space, and we have to go to space to save Earth. That's why this work is so important, and we don't have forever to do it. We've now gotten so big as a civilization on Earth that we kind of have to. I believe that really in a kind of a long timeframe, the most important work I'm doing is Blue Origin and pushing forward to get humanity established in the solar system.

Mark Bezos: What sort of timeframe are we talking about?

Jeff Bezos: Well, the grand vision, a trillion humans in the solar system and so on. I mean that's hundreds of years, but we can have in just a couple of decades a much lower-cost space travel, and then we can start to have a really dynamic entrepreneurial explosion in space. You can't really have much entrepreneurial activity in space today, because just the basic price of admission is too expensive. I mean just to do anything, even something relatively small in space is still very, very expensive. We need to lower the cost of admission so that thousands of entrepreneurs can have companies in space kind of like what we've seen on the internet. Right now, two kids in a dorm room can make Facebook, but they can't make a space company. It's not practical, I want to make that practical.

Mark Bezos: Gotcha. So and that leads me to think about some of the conversations we've had. This is another view of those mountains in West Texas, sitting around that fire place. Some of the most profound conversations for me anyway, that we've had are around the topic of long-term thinking.

Jeff Bezos: Yes.

Mark Bezos: Which is something that you've really embraced, and you've brought to the businesses that you run.

Jeff Bezos: Yes.

Mark Bezos: I was wondering if you could just talk a little bit, but I don't think that most people who are running businesses or who are even starting a company like Blue Origin, allow themselves to think in centuries, for a vision of what they're creating. At Amazon, I know that you've said five to seven-year timeframes for experiments that you're running. Talk to me about long-term thinking and your point of view on.

Jeff Bezos: Well, long-term thinking is a lever, it lets you do things that you could not do or couldn't even conceive of doing if you were thinking short term. So, that's why I have a project where I'm helping a group of people build the 10,000 year clock. Kind of ticks once a year and dongs once a century and the cuckoo comes out once a millennium. It's a bit of a big 500 foot tall thing.

Mark Bezos: Inside a mountain right here.

Jeff Bezos: Inside one of those mountains. The 10,000 year clock is a symbol. I don't think it will do anything for the first few hundred years, but after a few hundred years, once it's old, we will start to pay attention to older symbols. So in a few hundred years from now, I hope that people will think about that as a symbol for long-term thinking. If I collaborated with somebody here in this audience and I said, look, I want you to solve world hunger and I want you to do it in five years. You would properly reject the opportunity you would say, look, it's not possible, it's not practical. But if I said, look, I want you to solve world hunger in a hundred years, that's a job you'd take because it's a much more addressable problem.

You can first create the conditions where then you can solve the problem. So that's a very important way of thinking and I find it works with everything. I mean you have to back up and find the right time horizon for what you're trying to do, but at Amazon, we probably do most of our things, we expect that to get some results in sort of 5, 6, 7, 8 years. We find a lot of our other companies that compete against us in various ways, they're often trying to get things done in two or three years. If everything has to work in two to three years, then that limits what you can do. If you give yourself the breathing room to say I'm OK, if it takes seven years, all of a sudden you have way more opportunities.

Mark Bezos: One of the things I want to shift to here is when we are, raising a glass around the fire and you usually have a toast.

Jeff Bezos: To adventure and fellowship.

Mark Bezos: To adventure and fellowship and literally that's like little toast that he kicks off just about every dinner. You know it's interesting to me because I know that you are somebody who pays attention to the words that you use. You're careful about the words that you use and those seem like very specific words. I was wondering if we could just talk a little bit about why adventure and why fellowship. As I was thinking about this, it occurred to me that you've taken some adventures throughout your whole life.

Mark Bezos: People have asked me, because they know that we go on a lot of adventures together and they're a bit incredulous when I answer the question. They ask me, is he on his phone the whole time? Can he ever unplug? And they're incredulous when I say, honestly, he's not on his phone that much

I see the same thing when you're with your kids and it's how do you do that? I don't have a fraction of the responsibilities that you have and I find that I'm always wrestling with my phone. I'm just curious, like what sort of discipline or how do you go about compartmentalizing?

Jeff Bezos: I do not. So, like when I have dinner, I have dinner, whether it's with friends or with my family. I like to be talking to the people I'm with, I like to do whatever I'm doing, I don't like to multitask. It bothers me if I'm reading my email, I want to be really reading my email. When my mom tells a story about me being in Montessori school and they couldn't get me to switch tasks so my Montessori school teacher would have to literally pick up my chair and just move me to the next task station

I don't need discipline in order to not be checking my email. For me, it's very natural. I love being present in what I'm working and I'm happy multitasking, but I do it serially. Then honestly, if something really important is happening, somebody will find me. It's not like I have to check my text messages every five minutes or something like that, that's not a big deal.

Mark Bezos: Right. Usually when they do find you, it's rarely to give you good news.

Jeff Bezos: If somebody comes and says, you need to check your text messages right now, that's got to be bad news. It's usually a family thing or a medical thing or something. I think that it's probably just a very personal decision, some people are very good at multitasking and so they can do two things at once. When I am at a restaurant with my wife and we'll see a couple both texting, but every once in a while they've shown each other their phones and it seems like they're having a very nice date. I'm not sure there's anything wrong with that. It's just not how I'm wired.

Mark Bezos: Got it. So going back to the sense of adventure, can you talk to me a little bit about the role that adventure plays in your life and what is it that it brings to you? It's more than just a distraction.

Jeff Bezos: Yes, for me adventure is a, "you can choose." We all get to choose our life stories, it's the choices that define us, not our gifts. Everybody in this room has many gifts, I have many gifts. You can never be proud of your gifts because they were given to you. You might be tall, or you might be really good at math, you might be extremely beautiful or handsome, there are many gifts, but you can only be really proud of your choices, because those are the things that you are, that you are acting on.

One of the most important choices that each of us has and you know this just as well as I do, is you can choose a life of ease and comfort, or you can choose a life of service and adventure. When you're 80, which one of those things you think you're going to be more proud of? You're going to be more proud of having chosen a life of service and adventure. You see this in your firefighting work and everything else, you do Robin Hood and so on. For me adventure is a shorthand way of thinking about that.

Mark Bezos: Got it. I think that one of the other things that we've talked about when we talk about adventure is exposing yourself to new things and maintaining that childlike sense of wonder.

Jeff Bezos: Totally.

Mark Bezos: I know that this is important to you certainly in our personal lives, which is why we do all of these fun things. But it also plays an important role in how you approach the businesses that you're involved in.

Jeff Bezos: If you want to be an inventor of any kind, inventing a new service offering for customers, a new product or anything, being an inventor requires you to be a domain expert. I mean in a way, even if you're not at the beginning, you have to learn, learn, learn enough so that you become a domain expert. But the danger is once you become a domain expert, you can be trapped by that knowledge. So, inventors have this paradoxical ability to have that 10,000 hours of practice and be a real domain expert and have that beginner's mind. Have a look at it freshly, even though they know so much about the domain. That's the key to inventing, you have to have both. I think that is intentional, I think all of us have that inside of us and we can all do it, but you have to be intentional about it. You have to say, yes I am going to become an expert and I'm going to keep my beginner's mind.

Mark Bezos: I know that, I mean this is so important. It's a regular refrain, even at Amazon this far into it, it's still day one.

Jeff Bezos: Day one.

Mark Bezos: So I guess the other half of that toast is to fellowship.

Jeff Bezos: Yes.

Mark Bezos: Right to adventure and fellowship and again, fellowship is a very specific word. Friendship is much more common, so what is it about fellowship?

Jeff Bezos: For me, the word fellowship conjures the vision of traveling down the road together. It has more journey in it than friendship. Friendship is so great, and it would be great too, but fellowship captures friendship and traveling that path together.

Mark Bezos: Knowing how much time and effort you put into Amazon, The Washington Post and Blue Origin, I also happened to know that you're a devoted husband and beloved father with your kids. You have a fantastic relationship.

Jeff Bezos: The Bezos have a lot of kids. He has four. I have four our sister has three.

Mark Bezos: Yes.

Jeff Bezos: We're making sure that the population doesn't go down.

Mark Bezos: Well, one of the, I guess one of the questions I have is how do you go about establishing that work-life balance that everybody talks about and thinks about? I mean you live a big life how do you balance?

Jeff Bezos: I get this question a lot. I teach senior executive leadership classes at Amazon for our most senior executives. I also teach or speak to interns, so kind to all across the spectrum. I get this question about work-life balance all the time from both ends of the spectrum. My view is, I don't even like the phrase work-life balance, I think it's misleading. I like the phrase work-life harmony because I know that if I am energized at work, happy at work, feeling like I'm adding value, part of a team, whatever energizes you, that makes me better at home. It makes me a better husband, a better father and likewise, if I'm happy at home, it makes me a better employee, a better boss.

There may be crunch periods where it's about the number of hours, but that's not the real thing. Usually it's about, do you have energy? Is your work depriving you of energy or is your work generating energy for you? You know there are people, everybody in this room knows people who fall into these two camps. You're in a meeting and this person comes in the room. Some people come into the meeting, and they add energy to the meeting, other people come and the whole meeting just deflates. Those people drain energy from the meeting, and you have to decide which of those kinds of people you're going to be. Are you going to add energy?

Mark Bezos: Same thing at home.

Jeff Bezos: The same thing at home and so it's a wheel, it's a cycle. It's a flywheel, it's a circle, not a balance. That's why that metaphor is so dangerous because it implies there's a strict trade-off and you could be out of work, have all the time for your family, but really depressed and demoralized about your work situation and your family wouldn't want to be anywhere near you. They would wish you would take a vacation from them and so it's not about the number of hours, not primarily. I suppose if you went crazy with a hundred hours a week or something yes, that may be.

Mark Bezos: Right.

Jeff Bezos: Maybe there are limits and they probably are, but I've never had a problem and I think it's because both sides of my life give me energy and that's what I would recommend. That's what I do recommend to interns and execs.

Mark Bezos: So, we're out of time, I just want to say that first of all, thank you all for joining us. It brings me joy to have the opportunity to have conversations like this with you often. I do cherish those opportunities.

Jeff Bezos: Me too, brother. We should toast.

Mark Bezos: Yes. To adventure and fellowship.

Jeff Bezos: To adventure and fellowship.

Going to Space to Benefit Earth
(2019)

Replay of Apollo 11 Launch and Communication with Mission Control:

> "All engines running. Liftoff. We have a liftoff on Apollo 11. Tower cleared. Neil Armstrong reporting the role Pitch program. Would you put the Apollo 11 on a proper heading?
>
> Houston, Tranquility Base here, the Eagle has landed. As one small step for man, one giant leap for mankind. Will read the plaque that's on the front planting gear of this limb. There are two hemispheres, one showing each of the two hemispheres of Earth. Underneath it says, here men from the planet Earth, first set foot upon the moon, July 1969 AD. They came in peace for all mankind.
>
> Yes indeed, they've got the flag up now and you can see the stars and stripes."

Jeff Bezos: Wow! If that does not inspire you, you are at the wrong event. You don't choose your passions, your passions choose you. When I was five years old, I watched what you just watched, and it had a huge impact on me. It hasn't changed, none of that passion has gone away. This is me in high school, and I want to highlight this quote, 'The earth is finite, if the world economy and population are to keep expanding, space is the only way to go.' I still believe that. By the way, this is also my version of a misspent youth.

Guess what the best planet is in the solar system? It's easy to know the answer to that question. We've sent robotic probes like this one to all the planets in our solar system. Now some of them have been fly-bys, but we've examined them all. Earth is the best planet. It is not close. This one is really good. Don't even get me started on Venus.

Look at Earth, Earth is incredible. Jim Lovell, one of my real heroes on Apollo 8, while he was circling around the moon, he did something amazing. He put his thumb out and he realized with his thumb at arm's length, he could cover the whole Earth. Everything he'd ever known, he could cover with his thumb. He said something amazing, the old saying, 'I hope I go to heaven when I die.' He said, I realized at that that moment you go to heaven when you're born. Earth is heaven.

Carl Sagan, so poetic, on that blue dot, that's where everyone you know, and everyone you ever heard of, and every human being who ever lived, lived out their lives. A very small stage in a great cosmic arena. For all of human history, the earth has felt big to us, and actually in a really correct sense it has been big. Humanity has been small. That's not true anymore, the Earth is no longer big, humanity is big. It seems big to us, but it's finite, and there's something that we have to do. We have to realize that there are immediate problems. Things that we have to work on, and we are working on those things. They're urgent; I'm talking about poverty, hunger, homelessness, pollution, overfishing in the oceans.

This is a very long list of urgent, immediate problems and we need to work on those things urgently, in the here and now. But there are also long-range problems, and we need to work on those too. They take a long time to solve, you can't wait until the long-range problems are urgent to work on them. We can do both: we can and work on the here and now, and we can get started on the long-range problems. A very fundamental long-range problem is that we will run out of energy on earth. This is just arithmetic, it's going to happen.

As animals, humans use 97 watts of power. That's our metabolic rate as animals. But as members of the developed world, we use 10,000 Watts of power and we get a lot of benefit from it. We live in an era of dynamism and growth. You live better lives than your grandparents did, and your grandparents lived better lives than their grandparents did. And a big part of that is the abundance of energy that we've been able to harvest and use to our benefit. There are many good things that happen when we use energy.

When you go to the hospital, you're using a lot of energy. All the medical equipment that was manufactured for you. Transportation, the kinds of entertainments that we enjoy. The medications that we use, all of these things demand tremendous amount of energy, we don't want to stop using energy. But it is unsustainable, let me walk you through this. The historic rate of compounding of global energy usage is 3%

a year. Now 3% a year doesn't sound like very much, but over many years, the power of compounding is so extreme. 3% annual compounding is the equivalent of doubling human energy use every 25 years.

If you take global energy use today, you can power everything by covering Nevada in solar cells. Well, that seems challenging, but it also seems possible, and it is mostly desert anyway. But in just a couple of hundred years, at that 3% historic compounding rate, we'll have to cover the entire surface of the earth in solar cells. Now that's not going to happen, that's a very impractical solution and we can be sure it won't work. So what can we do? Well, one thing we can do is focus on efficiency and that is a good idea. The problem with it, is it's already assumed we've always been. As we've been growing, our energy use is 3% a year for centuries. We have been focusing on efficiency, let me give you some examples.

Two hundred years ago, you had to work 84 hours to afford one hour of artificial light. Today, you have to work 1.5 seconds to afford an hour of artificial light. We've moved from candles to oil lamps, to incandescent bulbs, to LEDs and gotten tremendous efficiency gains. Another example, transportation, air transport. In the 50 years, the half a century of commercial aviation, we've seen a 4X efficiency gain. Half a century ago, it took 109 gallons of fuel to fly one person across the country. Today in a modern 787, it takes only 24 gallons of fuel to fly a person across the country. It's an incredible improvement, it's very dramatic.

How about computation? We've seen a 1 trillion times increase in the efficiency of computation. The UNIVAC could do 15 calculations with one kilowatt second of energy. A modern processor can do 17 trillion calculations with one kilowatt second of energy. Now what happens when we get very efficient? We use more of these things. Artificial light has gotten very inexpensive, so we use a lot of it. Air transport has gotten very inexpensive, so we use it a lot of it. Computation has gotten very inexpensive, so we even have Snapchat. We have an ever-increasing demand for energy. We will become increasingly efficient and even in the face of that, we will be using more and more energy. That 3% compound growth rate already assumes great efficiency gains in the future.

What happens when unlimited demand meets finite resources? The answer is incredibly simple- rationing. That's the path that we would be on, and that path does not lead. It would lead for the first time to where your grandchildren and their grandchildren would have worse lives than you. That's a bad path. There's good news, the good news is that if we move out into the solar system, for all practical purposes, we have unlimited resources. So we get to choose, do we want stasis and rationing? Or do we want dynamism and growth. This is an easy choice. We know what we want, we just have to get busy. If we're out in the solar system, we can have a trillion humans in the source system. Which means we'd have a thousand Mozart and a thousand Einsteins. This would be an incredible civilization.

What could this future look like? Where would a trillion humans live? Well, it's very interesting, somebody named Jerry O'Neill, a physics professor looked at this question very carefully. He asked a very precise question that nobody had ever asked before. It was, is a planetary surface the best place for humans to expand into the solar system? He and his students set to work on answering that question and they came to a very surprising, for them, counterintuitive answer. No. Why not? Well, they came up with a bunch of problems: one is that other planetary surfaces aren't that big. You're talking about maybe a doubling at best, it's not that much, they're a long way away. Round trip times to Mars are on the order of years and launch opportunities to Mars are only once every 22 months, which is a very significant logistics problem.

Lastly, you're far enough away that you're not going to be able to do real-time communications with Earth. You're going to be limited by speed of light lag. The kids sitting here and probably some of the adults too, don't even think about playing Fortnite with somebody on Earth, that is not going to work. Most fundamentally, these other planetary surfaces do not have and cannot have Earth normal gravity. You're going to be stuck with whatever gravitational field they have. In the case of Mars, that's one third G. So instead, what O'Neil and his students came up with was the idea of manufactured worlds rotated to create artificial gravity with centrifugal force.

These are very large structures, miles on end, and they hold a million people or more each. Here's the International Space Station for scale. This is a very different kind of space colony.

Let's take a look at what they might look like inside. High-speed transport, agricultural areas, we added a little drone there. Cities in the background, some of them would be more recreational. They don't have to have the same gravity, you could have a recreational one that keeps zero G so that you can go flying with your own wings. Some would be national parks. These are really pleasant places to live, some of these O'Neill colonies might choose to replicate Earth cities. They might pick historical cities and mimic them in some way.

There'd be whole new kinds of architecture. These are ideal climates, these are shirtsleeve environments. This is Maui on its best day, all year long, no rain, no storms, snow earthquakes. What does the architecture even look like when it no longer has its primary purpose of shelter? We'll find out, but these are beautiful. People are going to want to live here, and they can be close to Earth so that you can return. Which is important because people are going to want to return to Earth. They're not going to want to leave Earth forever, they'll also be really easy to go between. The amount of energy required to go between these O'Neill colonies from one to another, to visit friends, to visit family, to visit one that's a recreational area. Very, very low energy needs to transport and quickly, it's a day trip.

This is a very interesting video clip I'm going to. This is Professor O'Neill, the guy who with his students came up with the idea of what's now called O'Neill Colonies and the famous science fiction author, Isaac Asimov, being interviewed about these colonies. Asimov gets asked a very good question, which is did anybody in science fiction ever predict this and if not, why not? He has a very good answer, watch this.

Interviewer: Did you anticipate anything like this in any of your science fiction?

Isaac Asimov: Nobody did really, because we've all been planet chauvinists. We've all believed people should live on the surface of a planet, of a world. I've had colonies on the moon, so have a hundred other science fiction writers. The closest I came to a manufactured world in free space was to suggest that we go out to the asteroid belt and hollow out the asteroids and make ships out of them. It never occurred to me to bring the material from the asteroids in, towards the earth where conditions are pleasant here and build the worlds there.

Jeff Bezos: Planetary chauvinist. All right, if we build this vision, these O'Neil colonies, where does it take us? What does it mean for earth? Earth ends up zoned residential and light industry. It will be a beautiful place to live, it'll be a beautiful place to visit. It'll be a beautiful place to go to college and to do some light industry. But heavy industry and all the polluting industry, all the things that are damaging our planet, those will be done off earth. We get to have both, we get to preserve this unique gem of a planet, which is completely irreplaceable. There is no plan B, we have to save this planet. We shouldn't give up a future for our grandchildren's grandchildren of dynamism and growth, we can have both.

Who is going to do this work? Not me. These kids in the front rows, you guys are going to do this, and your children are going to do this. This is going to take a long time, this is a big vision. What you're going to do is you're going to build whole industries. There are going to be thousands of future companies doing this work. A whole ecosystem of entrepreneurial activity unleashed, creative people coming up with new ideas about how to use space. But those companies, those entrepreneurial companies cannot exist today. It's impossible and the reason is the price of admission to do interesting things in space right now is just too high, because there's no infrastructure.

Let me tell you a story about Amazon. In 1994, I started Amazon. All of the heavy lifting infrastructure needed for Amazon to exist was already in place. We did not have to build a transportation system to deliver packages, it existed already. If we had had to build that, it would have been billions of dollars in capital, but it was there. It was called the US Postal Service and Deutsche Post and Royal Mail and UPS and FedEx. We got to stand on top of that infrastructure, the same thing with payment system, did we have to invent a payment system and roll that out? That would have been billions of dollars and many decades. But no, it already existed, it was called the credit card.

Do we have to deploy computers? No, they were already in most homes, mostly to play games. But they were there, that infrastructure already existed. Did we have to build a telecom network? That would have been billions of dollars, but we didn't. It was in place mostly to make long-distance phone calls and built by global telecom carriers like AT&T and their equivalents around the world. Infrastructure lets entrepreneurs do amazing things. So the kids here and your children and their grandchildren, you're going to build those O'Neill colonies. This generation's job, my generation's job is to build the infrastructure so that you'll be able to. We're going to build a road to space and then amazing things will happen. Then you'll see entrepreneurial creativity. Then you'll have space entrepreneurs start a company in their dorm room.

That can't happen today. So how really are we going to build O'Neill colonies? Nobody knows. I don't know. Nobody in this audience knows. That's for future generations to figure out the details. But what we can know is that there are certain gates we have to go through, certain precursors certain prerequisites. If we don't do these, we will never get there. It's really nice to know what those things are, cause you can work on them with great confidence that they're going to be useful. However, the details of that future vision evolve, these things are going to be essential. What are the two gates? First, we must have a radical reduction in launch cost. Launches are just simply too expensive today. Second, we have to use in space resources.

Earth has a very powerful gravitational field and lifting all of our resources off of earth, just isn't going to work. We need to be able to use the resources that are already in space. Here's New Shepard. The Blue Origin team has already made amazing progress on reusable launch vehicles. I'm incredibly proud of the work that this team has done. We now have 10 consecutive landings, we've used two boosters. Both have flown five times almost no refurbishment between flights. That's how you reduce launch costs, you have to have usable vehicles. Today, what we do is we use launch vehicles one time and throw them away. You also can't have fake reusability where you bring the vehicle back, but then do a lot of refurbishment. That also turns out to be very expensive.

We're going to be flying humans here in New Shepard this year, that's incredibly exciting. I want to talk to you about some of the architectural decisions that we made when we built New Shepard. New Shepard is a suborbital vehicle designed for space tourism. We made for that mission some very curious technology decisions. First of all, New Shepard is powered by liquid hydrogen. It is the highest performing rocket fuel, but it's also the most difficult to work with. It’s not needed for a suborbital mission. So why did we choose it? Because we knew we were going to need it for the next stage and we wanted to get practice with that hardest to use, but highest performing propellant. Same thing with vertical landing.

Why did we choose vertical landing for New Shepard? It's very counterintuitive actually. There are other landing mechanisms that would have worked at this scale. In fact, vertical landing gets easier the bigger the vehicle. Vertical landing is like balancing a broom on your fingertip. You can balance a broom, but try balancing a pencil, it's very challenging. The moment of inertia of the pencil is too small. So the great thing about vertical landing is it scales up really well. The bigger the vehicle, the easier it is. Right from the start, we wanted to build a human-rated system, so that we would be forced to think clearly about safety, reliability escape systems. All the things that we knew we would need to have practice within order to build our next generation of vehicles. So it's all about practice. I can't wait to start sending humans up in New Shepard later this year. It's a big deal. Thank you.

Let's talk about New Glenn, New Glenn is New Shepard's big brother. New Glenn is big enough that New Shepard will fit in the payload bay of New Glenn. It's 3.9 million pounds of thrust, it's a very large vehicle. I get asked a very interesting question from time to time that I like, and I enjoy, and I answer, and I play with. The question is Jeff, what's going to change over the next 10 years? That's a fun dinner conversation, but I'll tell you there's an even more important question that I almost never get asked, and that is what's not going to change over the next 10 years. The reason that question is so important is you can build your plans around those things.

At Amazon, I know for a fact, customers are going to want low prices, 10 years from now, that's not going to change. Customers are going to want fast delivery, they're going to want big selection. So all the energy we put into those things will continue to pay dividends. It is impossible to imagine a customer coming to me 10 years from now and saying Jeff, I love Amazon, I just wish you delivered a little more slowly. Or

I love Amazon, I just wish the prices were a little higher. It's not going to happen. So when you can figure out the things that are going to remain true under almost all circumstances, then you can put energy into them. We know what those things are for New Glenn. It's cost, reliability and on time launches. Right now, each one of those things needs improvement before we can go to this next phase of really going out into the solar system.

I know these things are stable in time. We are not going to have a New Glenn customer 10 years come to us and say, Jeff, I wish the rocket were just failed a little more often. Jeff, I wish that it was more expensive or that you were late on my launch dates. By the way the availability and launching on time is really a big problem in the industry and under appreciated by most people who aren't directly in the industry, it's really snarls things up and cost the payload customers a lot of money, all the delays. So these things won't change, we're going to put energy into them. The whole vehicle is designed around those three things. Here's a video to show you a little bit of what New Glenn will look like.

You can see the plume is a little bluish because it's powered by liquified natural gas as the fuel. Very inexpensive, 3.9 million pounds of liftoff thrust. You can see these big streaks on the end, that's to help the booster fly back to the landing ship. You're going to see separation, that's the second stage. It's powered by two of our BE3U engines. It's the same engine that's in New Shepard, the same liquid hydrogen engine in New Shepard, but an upper stage variant of it, and we'll deploy the payload. The first stage is designed to be reused 25 times. It has a seven-meter fairing, which is very large and that's important because a lot of payloads end up being volume constraint, rather than mass constraint.

It's a big vehicle, it'll lift 45 metric tons to Leo and 13 metric tons to GTO. It's geosynchronous transfer orbit. Here it is landing on the ship, the ship is underway when the vehicle lands. Why is the ship underway? Because we want really good weather availability. We're designing the system to be able to fly and launch payloads if the Orlando airport is open. We can't tell the customer, it looks good here, it's a nice day here at Cape Canaveral. But where we need to land our booster, we have heavy sea states. So with the ship that's underway, we can use fin stabilizers, stabilize that platform and operate this vehicle even in very heavy sea states. It’s designed for a human rating right from the very beginning. We'll fly it in 2021 for the first time.

So reusability is absolutely the key to radically reducing launch costs. People sometimes wonder how expensive is the fuel problem. Liquefied natural gas is very inexpensive, that's even though there are millions of pounds of propellant on New Glenn, the cost to fuel New Glenn with fuel and oxidizer, is less than a million dollars. That is not a significant cost in the scheme of things. The reason that launching things into orbit is so expensive today is because you throw the hardware away. It's like driving your car to the mall and then throwing it away after one trip. It's going to make trips to the mall very expensive. The second gate that I know we must go through,

I'm sure of it in space resources, we have to use them. We have a gift, we were given a gift, this nearby body called the moon.

We know a lot now about the moon that we didn't know back in the Apollo days, or even really just 20 years ago. One of the most important things we know about the moon today is that there's water there. It's in the form of ice, it's in the permanently shadowed craters on the poles of the moon and water is an incredibly valuable resource. You can use electrolysis to break down water into hydrogen and oxygen, and you have propellants. Another great thing about the moon, another reason it's a gift, it's nearby. It's three days away. You don't have constraints on launch the 22 months kind of thing that you have with Mars. You can go to the moon just about any time you want.

Of great importance for building large objects in space, the moon has six times less gravity than Earth. When you get resources from the moon, you can get them into free space at very low cost. It takes 24 times less energy to lift a pound off the moon than it does to lift a pound off the Earth. That is a huge lever, but guess what? The moon also needs infrastructure. Let me show you something. This is Blue Moon, we've been working on this Lander for three years. It's a very large Lander, it'll soft land in a precise way. 3.6 metric tons onto the lunar surface. The stretch tank variant of it will soft land, 6.5 metric tons onto the lunar surface. Let me give you a little tour.

The deck is designed to be a very simple interface, so that a great variety of payloads can be placed onto the top deck and secured. The davit system, which is inspired by naval systems, so you can see over here, is what's used to lower things off of the deck under the surface of the moon. The davits can be customized for the particular payloads. We have here's an example, a very large Rover, and by the way, even though that's a large Rover, this vehicle can land four of them simultaneously on the surface of the moon. If you go ahead and go back up on the deck again, let me show you a couple more things up there, some features. On the left-hand side, you can see our star tracker, so that this vehicle can autonomously navigate in space. There it is. On the right-hand side, you'll see an optical communication system that gives us gigabit bandwidth back to Earth. It's a laser that transmits data back to Earth. We also have X band for 10 megabit radio.

Let's keep going with the tour. Liquid hydrogen. Why are we using liquid hydrogen? This is not how Apollo did it. Why are we using liquid hydrogen as our fuel, a couple of reasons. One it's very high performance and so that helps a lot when you're landing on the moon, that's after you've got to carry all of your propellant to the moon. Second reason we're using liquid hydrogen is because ultimately we're going to be able to get hydrogen from that water on the moon and be able to refuel these vehicles on the surface of the moon and, use them. So liquid hydrogen is an excellent choice for fuel for the moon. We use it three ways on this vehicle, it's very interesting. The liquid hydrogen of course, is the fuel for the descent engine.

So it powers the descent, but we also use the boil off, so when liquid hydrogen heat seeps in through the tank walls.

Liquid hydrogen gasifies is a little bit it boils and that very cold gas is passed around the liquid oxygen tanks to prevent the liquid oxygen from boiling off. So that's the second use of the liquid hydrogen. Then after it has cooled the liquid oxygen tanks, it is pushed into an accumulator where it then powers hydrogen fuel cells. We chose hydrogen fuel cells for this vehicle rather than solar cells, because we want to be able to survive the lunar night, which you can't do with solar cells. The Lunar night is two weeks long and it gets very cold. Also the fuel cells provide a lot of power, it's two and a half kilowatts of power, which would be a very large solar array. Landing gear, they store an upward configuration so they can fit into the seven-meter payload bay. They deploy, they're designed to very wide splay angle. It is designed so that we can land on an incline on the moon of up to 15 degrees, which is a very big incline, be able to do that safely.

You can't see them there underneath here, but we have flash LIDAR, so we can do terrain mapping. There's no GPS on the moon. So if you want to land precisely and we can land within 75 feet of our target. When you want to land precisely, what you do is you use features on the moon to navigate. Now that we have mapped the entire moon in great detail, we can use that as preexisting maps to tell the system, it's a machine-learning system, to tell the system what it should be looking for in terms of craters and other features and it navigates relative to that, it uses the actual terrain of the moon as guideposts. This is an incredible vehicle and it's going to the moon. I have something else I'd like to show you

Jeff Bezos: This is a hard problem that we haven't yet, that needs still to be solved. This is very interesting. We were working on this for three years. This is the BE7 engine it's liquid hydrogen, liquid oxygen. We're going to hot fire it for the first time this summer, which is the only reason we can do that because we're working on it for three years. Most of it is printed. Has 10,000 pounds of thrust and it has very deep throttling capability. That's critical for a lunar descent engine because this Lander when it's fully loaded with fuel, which is 33,000 pounds/ when it's done it's decent burn and it's just about to land and the fuel is almost gone, it weighs less than 7,000 pounds.

So to provide the right amount of force on the vehicle with the engine, you need to be able to throttle it way down as the vehicle is getting lighter because it's burning its own fuel. Now, these problems that we're talking about, the kinds of things I'm talking about, we've solved them all already for New Shepard. It's very similar, the landing gear, liquid, hydrogen tanks, all of those things are solved. Even the autonomous descent and so on but we need the new engine and that's what this is. It's very exciting, the team has made incredible progress. We have an incredible propulsion team. I'm very proud of them and I can't wait to see it. 453 seconds of specific impulse, very high-performing engine. I can't wait for that first hot fire. I'm going to show a mission SIM. This is not a cartoon, this is real physics here. We've been simulating this for a long time. You'll note a couple of things. One thing is when this vehicle, there are payload bays here on the sides. When this vehicle is in orbit around the moon, has a kind of extra mission, a bonus mission. It can launch small satellites into orbit around the moon, so we can do certain kinds of science. You see it happening here, so we're deploying a number of small satellites before we do our landing. You're going to see the set of burns that will take us down to the surface. The primary burn is six minutes long, this BE7 engine will be firing for six minutes, it's a very long burn. That we verticalize about a kilometer above the surface, you can see that happening now.

A very precise landing again, using those flashlighters to detect surface features and using those for navigation. Now we're going to watch as the davit system, which is inspired by a naval system, deploys a Rover. Look at those long shadows, the shadows are always long on the poles of the moon. Wow! There's a lot of interesting science to be done on the moon, especially on the poles. We have formed a science advisory board there with us here today. Would you guys mind standing up just for one second to be recognized. Give these guys a hand, thank you. We appreciate it very much. The wisdom and advice from this group is going to make sure that the science gets done right and that we get the most bang for our buck doing that. Thank you.

We also have already a bunch of customers for Blue Moon, many of whom were in the audience. They're going to be deploying science missions to the moon as well. People are very excited about this capability to soft land their cargo, their rovers, their science experiments onto the surface of the moon in a precise way. There is no capability to do that today. Let's think about some other things we can put on top of this. Here's a picture of a pressurized human Rover, and it's really interesting when you can land precisely, you can configure missions that use multiple landings. So you send the Rover down first lowered onto the surface using the Davit system, make sure it's all in good working order and then send the astronauts. Speaking of sending the astronauts, here is a stretched tank version of what you see behind you. This is the stretch tank version of Blue Moon, which can soft land 6.5 metric tons onto the lunar surface, and this has an ascent vehicle on top.

I'll tell you one little thing that I think, just a little tiny anecdote. Do you see these landing gear? These pads, the foot pads. When I first saw the drawings of this a long time ago, I was like my images of Landers are all formed by the Apollo Lander. I was sure that those landing pads were too small, and I asked about that, and the answer is these are not too small. The ones on the lunar Apollo lander are too big because we were very worried about how soft the lunar surface was. It's just an example of how much more we know today. So these will work just fine, don't worry. Vice President Pence just recently said, it's the stated policy of this administration and the United States of America to return American astronauts to the moon within the next five years.

I love this, it's the right thing to do. For those of you doing the arithmetic at home, that's 2024 and we can help meet that timeline, but only because we started three years ago. It's time to go back to the moon, this time to stay. What I'm laying out here today, it's obviously a multi-generation vision, this is not going to get done by any one generation. One of the things that we have to do is inspire those future generations. So today, I'm announcing that Blue Origin is founding the club for the future, whose mission is to inspire young people to build the future of life and space. You see seated in front of you, the inaugural founding members of the club for the future. Thank you guys. We're going to do a series of activities focused on K through 12.

The first one I love, which is we're going to ask K through 12 students to send us postcards with their dreams of the future. Then we're going to send them to space in New Shepard and bring them back and mail them back to you. Today, I had the opportunity to meet with this group of kids just ahead of this presentation. Went over there about three o'clock while they were making their postcards and they're amazing! I saw several amazing ones, I really liked the one where the girl told me that on her, she had written the name of her crush at school that her mother doesn't yet know. I guess she assumes it's okay once we actually fly to space, by the time she gets this back, probably be okay. Mom can know at that point. I thought it was a very good plan.

By the way, if the kids I talked to earlier, these kids sitting in the front row, if they are representative of the current generation, we are in good shape. Teachers who want to participate in this with their kids, just come to the URL clubforfuture.org and it has all the instructions that you need. Please make no mistake about this, earth is the best planet. It isn't closed, we do need to protect. It's essential, it's our job. We're now big enough to hurt this planet. We have to use the resources of space. We must have a future for our grandchildren and their grandchildren of dynamism. We cannot let them fall prey to stasis and rationing. It’s this generation's job to build that road to space, so that the future generations can unleash their creativity.

When that is possible, when the infrastructure is in place, just as it was for me in 1994 to start Amazon. When we have that infrastructure in place for the future space entrepreneurs, you will see amazing things happen. It will happen fast, I guarantee it. People are so creative once they're unleashed. If this generation builds the road to space, builds that infrastructure, we will get to see thousands of future entrepreneurs building a real space industry. I want to inspire those future space entrepreneurs, I want you to think about this. This vision sounds very big, and it is, none of this is easy, all of it is hard. But I want to inspire you, and so think about this, big things start small.

Jeff Bezos Quotes

"We've had three big ideas at Amazon that we've stuck with for 18 years, and they're the reason we're successful: Put the customer first, invent and be patient."

"One of the things we don't do very well at Amazon is a me-too product offering. So when I look at physical retail stores, it's very well served, the people who operate physical retail stores are very good at it ... the question we would always have before we would embark on such a thing is: What's the idea? What would we do that would be different? How would it be better? We don't want to just do things because we can do them ... we don't want to be redundant."

"There are two kinds of companies, those that work to try to charge more and those that work to charge less. We will be the second."

"What we want to be is something completely new. There is no physical analog for what Amazon.com is becoming."

"We expect all our businesses to have a positive impact on our top and bottom lines. Profitability is very important to us or we wouldn't be in this business."

"If there's one reason we have done better than of our peers in the Internet space over the last six years, it is because we have focused like a laser on customer experience, and that really does matter, I think, in any business. It certainly matters online, where word-of-mouth is so very, very powerful."

"Friends congratulate me after a quarterly-earnings announcement and say, 'Good job, great quarter ... And I'll say, 'Thank you, but that quarter was baked three years ago. I'm working on a quarter that'll happen in 2021 right now.'"

"Amazon is not too big to fail ... If we start to focus on ourselves, instead of focusing on our customers, that will be the beginning of the end ... We have to try and delay that day for as long as possible."

"If everything you do needs to work on a three-year time horizon, then you're competing against a lot of people. But if you're willing to invest on a seven-year time horizon, you're now competing against a fraction of those people, because very few companies are willing to do that.

"At Amazon we like things to work in five to seven years. We're willing to plant seeds, let them grow and we're very stubborn. We say we're stubborn on vision and flexible on details."

In some cases, things are inevitable. The hard part is that you don't know how long it might take, but you know it will happen if you're patient enough. Ebooks had to happen.

Infrastructure web services had to happen. So you can do these things with conviction if you are long-term-oriented and patient.
"Amazon today remains a small player in global retail. We represent a low single-digit percentage of the retail market, and there are much larger retailers in every country where we operate. And that's largely because nearly 90% of retail remains offline, in brick and mortar stores."

"It's hard to remember for you guys, but for me it's like yesterday I was driving the packages to the post office myself, and hoping one day we could afford a forklift."

"I like treating things as if they're small, you know Amazon even though it is a large company, I want it to have the heart and spirit of a small one."

"Focus on cost improvement makes it possible for us to afford lower prices, which drives growth. Growth spreads fixed costs across more sales, reducing cost per unit, which makes possible more price reductions. Customers like this, and it's good for shareholders. Please expect us to repeat this loop."

"Wandering in business is not efficient ... but it's also not random. It's *guided* ... and powered by a deep conviction that the prize for customers is big enough that it's worth being a little messy and tangential to find our way there. Wandering is an essential counterbalance to efficiency. You need to employ both. The outsized discoveries – the "non-linear" ones – are highly likely to require wandering."

"Your margin is my opportunity."

"The balance of power is shifting toward consumers and away from companies... The right way to respond to this if you are a company is to put the vast majority of your energy, attention and dollars into building a great product or service and put a smaller amount into shouting about it, marketing it."

"The great thing about fact-based decisions is that they overrule the hierarchy."

"Market leadership can translate directly to higher revenue, higher profitability, greater capital velocity, and correspondingly stronger returns on invested capital."

"Part of company culture is path-dependent – it's the lessons you learn along the way."

"The killer app that got the world ready for appliances was the light bulb. So the light bulb is what wired the world. And they weren't thinking about appliances when they wired the world. They were really thinking about – they weren't putting electricity into the home. They were putting lighting into the home."

"The common question that gets asked in business is, 'why?' That's a good question, but an equally valid question is, 'why not?'"

"On the Internet, companies are scale businesses, characterized by high fixed costs and relatively low variable costs. You can be two sizes: You can be big, or you can be small. It's very hard to be medium. A lot of medium-sized companies had the financing rug pulled out from under them before they could get big."

"If you don't understand the details of your business, you are going to fail."

"I'm skeptical of any mission that has advertisers at its centerpiece."

"In the old world, you devoted 30% of your time to building a great service and 70% of your time to shouting about it. In the new world, that inverts."

"My own view is that every company requires a long-term view."

"A company shouldn't get addicted to being shiny, because shiny

“A word about corporate cultures: for better or worse, they are enduring, stable, hard to change. They can be a source of advantage or disadvantage. You can write down your corporate culture, but when you do so, you’re discovering it, uncovering it — not creating it.....The reason cultures are so stable in time is because people self-
“ ... seek to build a community–to make better choices in the people with whom you partner–that’s the only way to have greater long-term impact on the world.”

“I’d rather interview 50 people and not hire anyone than hire the wrong person.”

“During our hiring meetings, we ask people to consider three questions before making a decision ... Will you admire this person?...Will this person raise the average level of effectiveness of the group they’re entering?....Along what dimension might this person be a superstar?”

“I knew that if I failed I wouldn’t regret that, but I knew the one thing I might regret is not trying.”

“It is difficult for us to imagine that ten years from now, customers will want higher prices, less selection, or slower delivery. Our belief in the durability of these pillars gives us the confidence required to invest in strengthening them.”

"The most important single thing is to focus obsessively on the customer. Our goal is to be earth's most customer-centric company."

"Working backwards from customer needs can be contrasted with a "skills-forward" approach where existing skills and competencies are used to drive business opportunities. The skills-forward approach says, "We are really good at X. What else can we do with X?". However, if used exclusively, the company employing it will never be driven to develop fresh skills. Eventually the existing skills will become outmoded.
Working backwards from customer needs often demands that we acquire new competencies and exercise new muscles, never mind how uncomfortable and awkward feeling those first steps might be."

"One advantage — perhaps a somewhat subtle one — of a customer-driven focus is that it aids a certain type of proactivity. When we're at our best, we don't wait for external pressures. We are internally driven to improve our services, adding benefits and features, before we have to."

"We see our customers as invited guests to a party, and we are the hosts. It's our job every day to make every important aspect of the customer experience a little bit better."

"The best customer service is if the customer doesn't need to call you, doesn't need to talk to you. It just works."

"If your customer base is aging with you, then eventually you are going to become obsolete or irrelevant. You need to be constantly figuring out who are your new customers and what are you doing to stay forever young."

"If you're competitor-focused, you have to wait until there is a competitor doing something. Being customer-focused allows you to be more pioneering.

"I'm a big fan of all-you-can-eat plans, because they're simpler for customers."

"Our point of view is we will sell more if we help people make purchasing decisions."

"You don't want to negotiate the price of simple things you buy every day."

"The one thing that offends me the most is when I walk by a bank and see ads trying to convince people to take out second mortgages on their home so they can go on vacation. That's approaching evil."

"If you double the number of experiments you do per year, you're going to double your inventiveness."

"One of the only ways to get out of a tight box is to invent your way out."

"Things never go smoothly."

"There'll always be serendipity involved in discovery."

"Today I continue with my science-fiction reading habit and find it very mind-expanding. Always makes me think."

"The people who are right a lot often change their minds."

"There are two kinds of companies, those that work to try to charge more and those that work to charge less. We will be the second."

"A brand for a company is like a reputation for a person. You earn a reputation by trying to do hard things well."

"If you do build a great experience, customers tell each other about that. Word of mouth is very powerful."

"Obsess about customers, not competitors."

"I strongly believe that missionaries make better products. They care more. For a missionary, it's not just about the business."

"If you're good at course correcting, being wrong may be less costly ."

"All of my best decisions in business and in life have been made with heart, intuition, guts ... not analysis."

"If you can make a decision with analysis, you should do so. But it turns out in life that your most important decisions are always made with instinct and intuition, taste, heart."

"As a company grows, *everything* needs to scale, including the size of your failed experiments. If the size of your failures isn't growing, you're not going to be inventing at a size that can actually move the needle. Amazon will be experimenting at the right scale for a company of our size if we occasionally have multibillion-dollar failures."

"The good news for shareowners is that a single big winning bet can

"Because, you know, resilience – if you think of it in terms of the Gold Rush, then you'd be pretty depressed right now because the last nugget of gold would be gone. But the good thing is, with innovation, there isn't a last nugget. Every new thing creates two new questions and two new opportunities."

"I believe you have to be willing to be misunderstood if you're going to innovate."

"Invention is by its very nature disruptive. If you want to be understood at all times, then don't do anything new."

"Great industries are never made from single companies. There is room in space for a lot of winners."

"There has to be a business, and the business has to make sense, but that's not why you do it. You do it because you have something meaningful that motivates you."

"I believe you have to be willing to be misunderstood if you're going to innovate."

"My view is there's no bad time to innovate."

"I'm skeptical of any mission that has advertisers at its centerpiece."

"It's hard to find things that won't sell online."

"The common question that gets asked in business is, 'why?' That's a good question, but an equally valid question is, 'why not?'

"It's not an experiment if you know it's going to work."

"Work hard, have fun, and make history."

"Be stubborn on vision but flexible on details."

"It's perfectly healthy–encouraged, even–to have an idea tomorrow that contradicted your idea today."

"If you only do things where you know the answer in advance, your company goes away."

"Effective process is not bureaucracy. Bureaucracy is senseless process."

"When you receive criticism from well-meaning people, it pays to ask, 'Are they right?' And if they are, you need to adapt what they're doing. If they're not right ... you need to have that long-term willingness to be misunderstood."

"If you're not stubborn, you'll give up on experiments too soon. And if you're not flexible, you'll pound your head against the wall and you won't see a different solution to a problem you're trying to solve."

"The thing about inventing is you have to be both stubborn and flexible. The hard part is figuring out when to be which."

"What's dangerous is not to evolve, not to invent, not to improve the customer experience."

"I think frugality drives innovation, just like other constraints do. One of the only ways to get out of a tight box is to invent your way out."

"I believe you have to be willing to be misunderstood if you're going to innovate."

"There are two ways to extend a business. Take inventory of what you're good at and extend out from your skills. Or determine what your customers need and work backward, even if it requires learning new skills. Kindle is an example of working backward."

"It's not an experiment if you know it's going to work."

"If you decide that you're going to do only the things you know are going to work, you're going to leave a lot of opportunities on the table."

"There'll always be serendipity involved in discovery."

"If you're not stubborn, you'll give up on experiments too soon. And if you're not flexible, you'll pound your head against the wall and you won't see a different solution to a problem you're trying to solve."

"Life's too short to hang out with people who aren't resourceful."

"I don't want to use my creative energy on somebody else's user interface."

"The framework I found which made the decision incredibly easy was what I called – which only a nerd would call – a 'regret minimization framework.'
So I wanted to project myself forward to age 80 and say, 'Okay, now I'm looking back on my life. I want to have minimized the number of regrets I have."

"I don't think that you can invent on behalf of customers unless you're willing to think long-term, because a lot of invention doesn't work. If you're going to invent, it means you're going to experiment, and if you're going to experiment, you're going to fail, and if you're going to fail, you have to think long-term."

"You can do the math 15 different ways, and every time the math tells you that you shouldn't lower prices because you're going to make less money. That's undoubtedly true in the current quarter, in the current year.
But it's probably not true over a 10-year period, when the benefit is going to increase the frequency with which your customers shop with you, the fraction of their purchases they do with you as opposed to other places. Their overall satisfaction is going to go up."

"Another thing that I would recommend to people is that they always take a long-term point of view. I think this is something about which there's a lot of controversy. A lot of people — and I'm just not one of them — believe that you should live for the now.
I think what you do is think about the great expanse of time ahead of you and try to make sure that you're planning for that in a way that's going to leave you ultimately satisfied. This is the way it works for me. There are a lot of paths to satisfaction and you need to find one that works for you."

"You need a culture that high-fives small and innovative ideas and senior executives [that] encourage ideas. In order for innovative ideas to bear fruit, companies need to be willing to "wait for 5-7 years, and most companies don't take that time horizon."

"If you're very clear to the outside world that you're taking a long-term approach, then people can self-select in."

"I strongly believe that missionaries make better products. They care more. For a missionary, it's not just about the business. There has to be a business, and the business has to make sense, but that's not why you do it. You do it because you have something meaningful that motivates you."

"I think one thing I find very motivating — and I think this is probably a very common form of motivation or cause of motivation — is... I love people counting on me, and so, you know, today it's so easy to be motivated, because we have millions of customers counting on us at Amazon.com. We've got thousands of investors counting on us. And we're a team of thousands of employees all counting on each other. That's fun."

"The keys to success are patience, persistence, and obsessive attention to detail."

"I want to see good financial returns, but also to me there's the extra psychic return of having my creativity and technological vision bear fruit and change the world in a positive way."

"If you do build a great experience, customers tell each other about that. Word-of-mouth is very powerful."

"You know if you make a customer unhappy, they won't tell five friends, they'll tell 5,000 friends. So we are at a point now where we have all of the things we need to build an important and lasting company, and if we don't, it will be shame on us."

"If you make customers unhappy in the physical world, they might each tell 6 friends. If you make customers unhappy on the internet, they can each tell 6,000 friends."

"Your brand is what other people say about you when you're not in the room."

"A brand for a company is like a reputation for a person. You earn a reputation by trying to do hard things well."

Jeff Bezos Advice about Business and Life

If you don't love your work, you're never gonna be great at it. If you can get your work life to be where you enjoy half of it, that is amazing, very few people ever achieve that, because the truth is everything comes with overhead, that's reality. Everything comes with pieces that you don't like every job comes with pieces you don't like, and we need to say that's just part of it.

You have to figure out how to set up your life in such a way that you can minimize the things, and I find people don't dislike hard work. What people dislike and what is being out of control like they can't control their life they can't control their environment. This happens to me when I get over scheduled, I hate being over scheduled.

I want some time to be able to think and free myself. We all have the same amount of time in the world. Nobody has more time than anybody else and when you become a very successful person, one of the things you start to get over scheduled.

The other thing I would suggest to any young person, even before they start their career, is to really think about their choices, because I find young people - and I, when I was young, made this mistake too.

You can get very fixed on your gifts, so everybody has gifts, you know you have gifts and you have things that you didn't get gifted. Maybe you're extremely beautiful, maybe you're extremely good at mathematics, there are a lot of things that you can be given, but those things can confuse you because they're not the things that construct your life. It's your choices that construct your life, not your gifts. You can celebrate your gifts, be proud of them, be happy of them. Actually, don't be proud of them, be celebratory of them, you can't be proud because they're gifts. They were given to you, you didn't earn them. You can only be proud of the things you earn, and so, as I got older, I started to realize I wasn't proud of my gifts.

I was always good at school. School was always easy for me, and I was always proud that I was a great student. I got A's in all my classes. I was good at math. I thought that's who I was, but it's not true. Those are the things that are gifts. What was hard for me is deciding to work hard, deciding to use my gifts in certain ways to challenge myself. To do things that I didn't think I could do, to put myself in uncomfortable situations.

You can choose a life of ease and comfort or you can choose a life of service and adventure, which one of those when you're 90 years old, are you going to be more proud of.
How will you use your gifts?
What choices will you make?
Will inertia, be your guide, or will you follow your passions?
Will you follow dogma or will you be original?

Will you wilt under criticism, or will you follow your convictions?
Will you bluff it out when you're wrong or will you apologize?
Will you guard your heart against rejection or react when you fall in love?
Will you play it safe, or will you be a little bit swashbuckling when it's tough?
Will you give up or will you be relentless?
Will you be a cynic, or will you be a builder?
Will you be clever at the expense of others, or will you be kind?
Tomorrow and in a quiet moment of reflection, narrating for only yourself the most personal version of your life story, the telling that will be most compact and meaningful will be the series of choices you have made in the end.

We are our choices, build yourself, a great story.

I think everybody has their own passion their own thing that they're interested in, and then you are, very alert to the things that are in the sphere of influence of that passion.

Do something you're very passionate about and don't try to chase what is kind of the hot passion of the day. You guys will find that you have passions and having a passion is a gift. I think we all have passions and you don't get to choose them, they pick you, but you have to be alert to them. You have to be looking for them and when you find your passion, it's a fantastic gift for you, because it gives you direction, it gives you purpose.

My advice would be the same for any kind of entrepreneur, and that is making sure that you are focused on something you're passionate about.

You could have a job, you can have a career or you can have a calling, and the best thing is to have a calling. If you find your passion, all your work won't feel like work to you.

Many kids and many grown-ups do figure out over time what their passions are. Sometimes what happens is that we let our intellectual selves overrule those passions and so that's what needs to be guarded against.

One of my jobs as the leader of Amazon is to encourage people to be bold and people love to focus on things that aren't yet working and that's good, it's human nature.
That kind of divine discontent can be very helpful, but really it's incredibly hard to get people to take bold bets, and you need to encourage that.

Every single important thing we've ever done. The most important things have always seemed dumb to industry experts at the beginning, so you have to get really good results. You have to defy conventional wisdom.

You are going to take bold bets, they're going to be experiments and if they are experiments, you don't know ahead of time if they're going to work. Experiments are by their very nature prone to failure, but big success a few big successes, compensate for dozens and dozens of things that didn't work. So you know bold bets like AWS, Kindle, Amazon Prime, our 3rd party seller business. All of those things are examples of bull bets that did work and they pay for a lot of experiments.

I have made billions of dollars of failures at amazon.com literally billions of dollars of failures, you might remember Pets.com or Cosmo, or Give myself a root canal with no anesthesia very easily. None of those things are fun, but they don't matter. What really matters is companies that don't continue to experiment, companies that don't embrace failure. They eventually get in the desperate position where the only thing they can do is a kind of Hail Mary bet at the very end of their corporate existence.

You can be out of work and have terrible work-life balance, even though you've got all the time in the world. You could just feel like, oh my God, I'm miserable, you would be draining energy, and so you have to find that harmony, it's a much better word.

Stress comes from ignoring things that you shouldn't be ignoring. I think in large part, people get stressed wrong all the time, in my opinion, stress doesn't come from hard work. For example, you can be working incredibly hard and loving it, and likewise you can be out of work and incredibly stressed over that, no matter how good we are, we can still be better. The stress primarily comes from not taking action over something that you can have some control over. You can always be better

I think for most people it's about meaning, people want to know that they're doing something interesting and useful. For us because of the challenges that we have chosen for ourselves, we get to work in the future, it's super fun to work in the future for the right kind of person.

You need to be nimble and robust, you need to be able to take a punch, you also need to be quick and innovative and doing new things at a high speed. That's the best defense against the future, you have to always be leaning into the future. If you're leaning away from the future, the future is gonna win every time. Never ever lean away from the future.

We all have adversity in our lives, there's no lack of adversity and by the way that's good, because it's what teaches us how to get back up. You fall down, you get back up, it always happens.

You get certain gifts in life and you want to take advantage of those, but I guess my advice on adversity and success would

be to be proud not of your gifts, but of your hard work and your choices.
The kinds of gifts you get like you might be really good at math, it might be really easy for you that's a kind of a gift, but practicing that math and taking it to the next step, that could be very challenging and take a lot of sweat that's a choice. But you can't really be proud of your gifts because they were given to you. You can be grateful for them and thankful for them, but your choices when you choose to work hard, or to do hard things, those are choices that you can be proud of.

Being an inventor requires, because the world is so complicated, to be a domain expert. I mean in a way, even if you're not at the beginning, you have to learn, learn, learn enough, so to become a domain expert, but the danger is once you've become a domain expert, you can be trapped by that knowledge and so inventors have this paradoxical ability to have that 10,000 hour of practice and be a real domain expert and have that beginner's mind. Have that look at it freshly, even though they know so much about the domain and that's the key to inventing, you have to have both - and I think that is intentional.

I think all of us have that inside of us and we can all do it, but you have to be intentional about it. You have to say yeah, I am going to become an expert and I'm gonna keep my beginner's mind, you can't skip steps.

You have to put one foot in front of the other, things take time, there are no shortcuts, but you want to do those steps with passion and ferocity. It's easy to have ideas, but it's very hard to turn an idea into a successful product.
There are a lot of steps in between, it takes persistence, relentlessness, so I always tell people who think they want to be entrepreneurs is, you need a combination of stubbornness, relentlessness and flexibility and you have to know when and how to use them.

Basically, you need to be stubborn on your vision, because otherwise it'll be too easy to give up. You need to be very flexible on the details because, as you go along pursuing your vision, you'll find that some of your preconceptions were wrong. You're going to need to be able to change those things, so I think, taking an idea successfully all the way to the market and turning it into a real product that people care about and that really improves people's lives is a lot of hard work.

Customers have a divine discontent and they teach you if you listen to them. So we watch for that and we see patterns and we can find places where it's, not working something's going wrong and that's.

Really, how I get the feedback is from customer input. What you really want to do is you take that it's, an anecdote. It's, a single example, but you need to find the root cause. What went wrong deep inside the system? How did this happen? Because then you can fix it for everyone.

You don't just fix the symptom, you have to fix the root cause and that's been the secret to our operational success for 20 years. There are a lot of things that are a waste of time.

Don't try to chase what is kind of the hot passion of the day. I think you see it all over the place in many different contexts, we saw it in the internet world quite a bit where at the peak of the internet mania say in 1999, you found people who were very passionate, they kind of left that job and decided they could do something in the internet because it was almost like the 1849 Gold Rush in a way.
They might have been a doctor, but they quit and started panning for gold and that almost never works, and even if it does work, according to some metrics, financial success can leave you ultimately unsatisfied, so you really need to be very clear with yourself.

I think one of the best ways to do that is this notion of projecting yourself forward to age 80. Looking back on your life and trying to make sure you've minimized the number of regrets you have, that works for career decisions, it works for family decisions. I have a 14 month old son and it's very easy for me to think about myself, when I'm 80, I know I want to watch that little guy grow up, and so, I don't want to be 80 and think shoot, I missed that whole thing and I don't have the kind of relationship with my son that I wished I had. And so on.

I guess another thing that I would recommend to people is that they always take a long-term point of view, I think this is something about which there's a lot of controversy.

You know there are a lot of people, I'm just not one of them, believe that you should live for the now. I think what to do is think about the great expanse of time ahead of you and try to make sure that you're planning for that in a way that's gonna leave you ultimately satisfied.
This is the way that works for me, I think everybody needs to find that for themselves? There are a lot of paths to satisfaction and you need to find one that works for you.

Opening Remarks to Congress

Ahead of Antitrust Hearing (2020)

I'm Jeff Bezos. I founded Amazon 26 years ago with the long-term mission of making it Earth's most customer-centric company.
My mom, Jackie, had me when she was a 17-year-old high school student in Albuquerque, New Mexico. Being pregnant in high school was not popular in Albuquerque in 1964. It was difficult for her. When they tried to kick her out of school, my grandfather went to bat for her. After some negotiation, the principal said, "OK, she can stay and finish high school, but she can't do any extracurricular activities, and she can't have a locker." My grandfather took the deal, and my mother finished high school, though she wasn't allowed to walk across the stage with her classmates to get her diploma. Determined to keep up with her education, she enrolled in night school, picking classes led by professors who would let her bring an infant to class. She would show up with two duffel bags—one full of textbooks, and one packed with diapers, bottles, and anything that would keep me interested and quiet for a few minutes.

My dad's name is Miguel. He adopted me when I was four years old. He was 16 when he came to the United States from Cuba as part of Operation Pedro Pan, shortly after Castro took over. My dad arrived in America alone. His parents felt he'd be safer here. His mom imagined America would be cold, so she made him a jacket sewn entirely out of cleaning cloths, the only material they had on hand. We still have that jacket; it hangs in my parents' dining room. My dad spent two weeks at Camp Matecumbe, a refugee center in Florida, before being moved to a Catholic mission in Wilmington, Delaware. He was lucky to get to the mission, but even so, he didn't speak English and didn't have an easy path. What he did have was a lot of grit and determination. He received a scholarship to college in Albuquerque, which is where he met my mom. You get different gifts in life, and one of my great gifts is my mom and dad. They have been incredible role models for me and my siblings our entire lives.

You learn different things from your grandparents than you do from your parents, and I had the opportunity to spend my summers from ages four to 16 on my grandparents' ranch in Texas. My grandfather was a civil servant and a rancher—he worked on space technology and missile- defense systems in the 1950s and '60s for the Atomic Energy Commission—and he was self- reliant and resourceful. When you're in the middle of nowhere, you don't pick up a phone and call somebody when something breaks. You fix it yourself. As a kid, I got to see him solve many seemingly unsolvable problems himself, whether he was restoring a broken-down Caterpillar bulldozer or doing his own veterinary work. He taught me that you can take on hard problems. When you have a setback, you get back up and try again. You can invent your way to a better place.

I took these lessons to heart as a teenager, and became a garage inventor. I invented an automatic gate closer out of cement-filled tires, a solar cooker out of an umbrella and tinfoil, and alarms made from baking pans to entrap my siblings.

The concept for Amazon came to me in 1994. The idea of building an online bookstore with millions of titles—something that simply couldn't exist in the physical world—was exciting to me. At the time, I was working at an investment firm in New York City.

When I told my boss I was leaving, he took me on a long walk in Central Park. After a lot of listening, he finally said, "You know what, Jeff, I think this is a good idea, but it would be a better idea for somebody who didn't already have a good job." He convinced me to think about it for two days before making a final decision. It was a decision I made with my heart and not my head. When I'm 80 and reflecting back, I want to have minimized the number of regrets that I have in my life. And most of our regrets are acts of omission—the things we didn't try, the paths untraveled.

And I decided that if I didn't at least give it my best shot, I was going to regret not trying to participate in this thing called the internet that I thought was going to be a big deal.

The initial start-up capital for Amazon.com came primarily from my parents, who invested a large fraction of their life savings in something they didn't understand. They weren't making a bet on Amazon or the concept of a bookstore on the internet. They were making a bet on their son. I told them that I thought there was a 70% chance they would lose their investment, and they did it anyway. It took more than 50 meetings for me to raise $1 million from investors, and over the course of all those meetings, the most common question was, "What's the internet?"

Unlike many other countries around the world, this great nation we live in supports and does not stigmatize entrepreneurial risk-taking. I walked away from a steady job into a Seattle garage to found my startup, fully understanding that it might not work. It feels like just yesterday I was driving the packages to the post office myself, dreaming that one day we might be able to afford a forklift.

Amazon's success was anything but preordained. Investing in Amazon early on was a very risky proposition. From our founding through the end of 2001, our business had cumulative losses of nearly $3 billion, and we did not have a profitable quarter until the fourth quarter of that year. Smart analysts predicted Barnes & Noble would steamroll us, and branded us "Amazon.toast." In 1999, after we'd been in business for nearly five years, Barron's headlined a story about our impending demise "Amazon.bomb." My annual shareholder letter for 2000 started with a one- word sentence: "Ouch."

At the pinnacle of the internet bubble our stock price peaked at $116, and then after the bubble burst our stock went down to $6. Experts and pundits thought we were going out of business. It took a lot of smart people with a willingness to take a risk with me, and a willingness to stick to our convictions, for Amazon to survive and ultimately to succeed. And it wasn't just those early years. In addition to good luck and great people, we have been able to succeed as a company only because we have continued to take big risks. To invent you have to experiment, and if you know in advance that it's going to work, it's not an experiment. Outsized returns come from betting against conventional wisdom, but conventional wisdom is usually right.

A lot of observers characterized Amazon Web Services as a risky distraction when we started. "What does selling compute and storage have to do with selling books?" they wondered. No one asked for AWS. It turned out the world was ready and hungry for cloud computing but didn't know it yet. We were right about AWS, but the truth is we've also taken plenty of risks that didn't pan out. In fact, Amazon has made billions of dollars of failures. Failure inevitably comes along with invention and risk-taking, which is why we try to make Amazon the best place in the world to fail.
Since our founding, we have strived to maintain a "Day One" mentality at the company. By that I mean approaching everything we do with the energy and entrepreneurial spirit of Day One. Even though Amazon is a large company, I have

always believed that if we commit ourselves to maintaining a Day One mentality as a critical part of our DNA, we can have both the scope and capabilities of a large company and the spirit and heart of a small one.

In my view, obsessive customer focus is by far the best way to achieve and maintain Day One vitality. Why? Because customers are always beautifully, wonderfully dissatisfied, even when they report being happy and business is great. Even when they don't yet know it, customers want something better, and a constant desire to delight customers drives us to constantly invent on their behalf. As a result, by focusing obsessively on customers, we are internally driven to improve our services, add benefits and features, invent new products, lower prices, and speed up shipping times—before we have to. No customer ever asked Amazon to create the Prime membership program, but it sure turns out they wanted it. And I could give you many such examples. Not every business takes this customer-first approach, but we do, and it's our greatest strength.

Customer trust is hard to win and easy to lose. When you let customers make your business what it is, then they will be loyal to you—right up to the second that someone else offers them better service. We know that customers are perceptive and smart.

We take as an article of faith that customers will notice when we work hard to do the right thing, and that by doing so again and again, we will earn trust. You earn trust slowly, over time, by doing hard things well— delivering on time; offering everyday low prices; making promises and keeping them; making principled decisions, even when they're unpopular; and giving customers more time to spend with their families by inventing more convenient ways of shopping, reading, and automating their homes.

As I have said since my first shareholder letter in 1997, we make decisions based on the long-term value we create as we invent to meet customer needs. When we're criticized for those choices, we listen and look at ourselves in the mirror. When we think our critics are right, we change. When we make mistakes, we apologize. But when you look in the mirror, assess the criticism, and still believe you're doing the right thing, no force in the world should be able to move you.

Fortunately, our approach is working. Eighty percent of Americans have a favorable impression of Amazon overall, according to leading independent polls. Who do Americans trust more than Amazon "to do the right thing?" Only their primary physicians and the military, according to a January 2020 Morning Consult survey. Researchers at Georgetown and New York University found in 2018 that Amazon trailed only the military among all respondents to a survey on institutional and brand trust. Among Republicans, we trailed only the military and local police; among Democrats, we were at the top, leading every branch of government, universities, and the press. In Fortune's 2020 rankings of the World's Most Admired Companies, we came in second place (Apple was #1). We are grateful that customers notice the hard work we do on their behalf, and that they reward us with their trust. Working to earn and keep that trust is the single biggest driver of Amazon's Day One culture.

The company most of you know as Amazon is the one that sends you your online orders in the brown boxes with the smile on the side. That's where we started, and retail remains our largest business by far, accounting for over 80% of our total revenue.

The very nature of that business is getting products to customers. Those operations need to be close to customers, and we can't outsource these jobs to China or anywhere else. To fulfill our promises to customers in this country, we need American workers to get products to American customers.
When customers shop on Amazon, they are helping to create jobs in their local communities. As a result, Amazon directly employs a million people, many of them entry-level and paid by the hour. We don't just employ highly educated computer scientists and MBAs in Seattle and Silicon Valley.

We hire and train hundreds of thousands of people in states across the country such as West Virginia, Tennessee, Kansas, and Idaho. These employees are package stowers, mechanics, and plant managers. For many, it's their first job. For some, these jobs are a stepping stone to other careers, and we are proud to help them with that. We are spending more than $700 million to give more than 100,000 Amazon employees access to training programs in fields such as healthcare, transportation, machine learning, and cloud computing. That program is called Career Choice, and we pay 95% of tuition and fees toward a certificate or diploma for in- demand, high-paying fields, regardless of whether it's relevant to a career at Amazon.

Patricia Soto, one of our associates, is a Career Choice success story. Patricia always wanted to pursue a career in the medical field to help care for others, but with only a high school diploma and facing the costs of post-secondary education, she wasn't sure she'd be able to accomplish that goal.

After earning her medical certification through Career Choice, Patricia left Amazon to start her new career as a medical assistant at Sutter Gould Medical Foundation, supporting a pulmonary medicine doctor. Career Choice has given Patricia and so many others a shot at a second career that once seemed out of reach.

Amazon has invested more than $270 billion in the U.S. over the last decade. Beyond our own workforce, Amazon's investments have created nearly 700,000 indirect jobs in fields like construction, building services, and hospitality. Our hiring and investments have brought much- needed jobs and added hundreds of millions of dollars in economic activity to areas like Fall River, Massachusetts, California's Inland Empire, and Rust Belt states like Ohio. During the COVID-19 crisis, we hired an additional 175,000 employees, including many laid off from other jobs during the economic shutdown.

We spent more than $4 billion in the second quarter alone to get essential products to customers and keep our employees safe during the COVID-19 crisis. And a dedicated team of Amazon employees from across the company has created a program to regularly test our workers for COVID-19. We look forward to sharing our learnings with other interested companies and government partners.

The global retail market we compete in is strikingly large and extraordinarily competitive. Amazon accounts for less than 1% of the $25 trillion global retail market and less than 4% of retail in the U.S. Unlike industries that are winner-take-all, there's room in retail for many winners. For example, more than 80 retailers in the U.S. alone earn over $1 billion in annual revenue. Like any retailer, we know that the success of our store depends entirely on customers' satisfaction with their experience in our store. Every day, Amazon competes against large, established players like Target, Costco, Kroger, and, of course, Walmart—a company more than twice Amazon's size.

And while we have always focused on producing a great customer experience for retail sales done primarily online, sales initiated online are now an even larger growth area for other stores. Walmart's online sales grew 74% in the first quarter. And customers are increasingly flocking to services invented by other stores that Amazon still can't match at the scale of other large companies, like curbside pickup and in-store returns.

The COVID-19 pandemic has put a spotlight on these trends, which have been growing for years. In recent months, curbside pickup of online orders has increased over 200%, in part due to COVID- 19 concerns. We also face new competition from the likes of Shopify and Instacart—companies that enable traditionally physical stores to put up a full online store almost instantaneously and to deliver products directly to customers in new and innovative ways—and a growing list of omnichannel business models. Like almost every other segment of our economy, technology is used everywhere in retail and has only made retail more competitive, whether online, in physical stores, or in the various combinations of the two that make up most stores today. And we and all other stores are acutely aware that, regardless of how the best features of "online" and "physical" stores are combined, we are all competing for and serving the same customers. The range of retail competitors and related services is constantly changing, and the only real constant in retail is customers' desire for lower prices, better selection, and convenience. It's also important to understand that Amazon's success depends overwhelmingly on the success of the thousands of small and medium-sized businesses that also sell their products in Amazon's stores.

Back in 1999, we took what at the time was the unprecedented step of welcoming third-party sellers into our stores and enabling them to offer their products right alongside our own. Internally, this was extremely controversial, with many disagreeing and some predicting this would be the beginning of a long, losing battle.
We didn't have to invite third-party sellers into the store. We could have kept this valuable real estate for ourselves. But we committed to the idea that over the long term it would increase selection for customers, and that more satisfied customers would be great for both third-party sellers and for Amazon. And that's what happened. Within a year of adding those sellers, third-party sales accounted for 5% of unit sales, and it quickly became clear that customers loved the convenience of being able to shop for the best products and to see prices from different sellers all in the same store. These small and medium-sized third-party businesses now add significantly more product selection to Amazon's stores than Amazon's own retail operation. Third-party sales now account for approximately 60% of physical product sales on Amazon, and those sales are growing faster than Amazon's own retail sales. We guessed that it wasn't a zero sum game. And we were right—the whole pie did grow, third-party sellers did

very well and are growing fast, and that has been great for customers and for Amazon.

There are now 1.7 million small and medium-sized businesses around the world selling in Amazon's stores. More than 200,000 entrepreneurs worldwide surpassed $100,000 in sales in our stores in 2019. On top of that, we estimate that third-party businesses selling in Amazon's stores have created over 2.2 million new jobs around the world.

One of those sellers is Sherri Yukel, who wanted to change careers to be home more for her children. She started handcrafting gifts and party supplies for friends as a hobby, and eventually began selling her products on Amazon. Today, Sherri's company employs nearly 80 people and has a global customer base. Another is Christine Krogue, a stay-at-home mother of five in Salt Lake City. Christine started a business selling baby clothes through her own website before taking a chance on Amazon. She has since seen her sales more than double, and she's been able to expand her product line and hire a team of part-time employees. Selling on Amazon has allowed Sherri and Christine to grow their own businesses and satisfy customers on their own terms.

And it is striking to remember how recent all of this is. We did not start out as the largest marketplace—eBay was many times our size. It was only by focusing on supporting sellers and giving them the best tools we could invent that we were able to succeed and eventually surpass eBay. One such tool is Fulfillment by Amazon, which enables our third-party sellers to stow their inventory in our fulfillment centers, and we take on all logistics, customer service, and product returns.

By dramatically simplifying all of those challenging aspects of the selling experience in a cost-effective way, we have helped many thousands of sellers grow their businesses on Amazon. Our success may help explain the wide proliferation of marketplaces of all types and sizes around the world. This includes U.S. companies like Walmart, eBay, Etsy, and Target, as well as retailers based overseas but selling globally, such as Alibaba and Rakuten. These marketplaces further intensify competition within retail.
The trust customers put in us every day has allowed Amazon to create more jobs in the United States over the past decade than any other company—hundreds of thousands of jobs across 42 states. Amazon employees make a minimum of $15 an hour, more than double the federal minimum wage (which we have urged Congress to increase).

We've challenged other large retailers to match our $15 minimum wage. Target did so recently, and just last week so did Best Buy. We welcome them, and they remain the only ones to have done so. We do not skimp on benefits, either. Our full-time hourly employees receive the same benefits as our salaried headquarters employees, including comprehensive health insurance starting on the first day of employment, a 401(k) retirement plan, and parental leave, including 20 weeks of paid maternity leave. I encourage you to benchmark our pay and benefits against any of our retail competitors.

More than 80% of Amazon shares are owned by outsiders, and over the last 26 years—starting from zero—we've created more than $1 trillion of wealth for those outside shareholders. Who are those shareowners? They are pension funds: fire, police, and school teacher pension funds. Others are 401(k)s—mutual funds that own pieces of Amazon. University endowments, too, and the list goes on. Many people will retire better because of the wealth we've created for so many, and we're enormously proud of this. At Amazon, customer obsession has made us what we are, and allowed us to do ever greater things. I know what Amazon could do when we were 10 people. I know what we could do when we were 1,000 people, and when we were 10,000 people. And I know what we can do today when we're nearly a million.

I love garage entrepreneurs—I was one. But, just like the world needs small companies, it also needs large ones. There are things small companies simply can't do. I don't care how good an entrepreneur you are, you're not going to build an all-fiber Boeing 787 in your garage.
Our scale allows us to make a meaningful impact on important societal issues. The Climate Pledge is a commitment made by Amazon and joined by other companies to meet the goals of

the Paris Agreement 10 years early and be net zero carbon by 2040. We plan to meet the pledge, in part, by purchasing 100,000 electric delivery vans from Rivian—a Michigan-based producer of electric vehicles.

Amazon aims to have 10,000 of Rivian's new electric vans on the road as early as 2022, and all 100,000 vehicles on the road by 2030. Globally, Amazon operates 91 solar and wind projects that have the capacity to generate over 2,900 MW and deliver more than 7.6 million MWh of energy annually—enough to power more than 680,000 U.S. homes. Amazon is also investing $100 million in global reforestation projects through the Right Now Climate Fund, including $10 million Amazon committed in April to conserve, restore, and support sustainable forestry, wildlife and nature-based solutions across the Appalachian Mountains—funding two innovative projects in collaboration with The Nature Conservancy. Four global companies—Verizon, Reckitt Benckiser, Infosys, and Oak View Group—recently signed The Climate Pledge, and we continue to encourage others to join us in this fight. Together, we will use our size and scale to address the climate crisis right away. And last month, Amazon introduced The Climate Pledge Fund, started with $2 billion in funding from Amazon.

The Fund will support the development of sustainable technologies and services that in turn will enable Amazon and other companies to meet The Climate Pledge. The Fund will invest in visionary entrepreneurs and innovators who are

building products and services to help companies reduce their carbon impact and operate more sustainably.
We recently opened the largest homeless shelter in Washington state—and it's located inside one of our newest headquarters buildings in downtown Seattle. The shelter is for Mary's Place, an incredible Seattle-based nonprofit. The shelter, part of Amazon's $100 million investment in Mary's Place, spans eight floors and can accommodate up to 200 family members each night. It has its own health clinic and provides critical tools and services to help families fighting homelessness get back on their feet. And there is dedicated space for Amazon to provide weekly pro-bono legal clinics offering counsel on credit and debt issues, personal injury, housing and tenant rights. Since 2018, Amazon's legal team has supported hundreds of Mary's Place guests and volunteered more than 1,000 pro-bono hours.

Amazon Future Engineer is a global childhood-to-career program designed to inspire, educate, and prepare thousands of children and young adults from underrepresented and underserved communities to pursue a computer science career. The program funds computer science coursework and professional teacher development for hundreds of elementary schools, introductory and AP Computer Science classes for more than 2,000 schools in underserved communities across the country, and 100 four-year, $40,000 college scholarships to computer science students from low-income backgrounds. Those scholarship recipients also receive guaranteed internships at Amazon.

There is a diversity pipeline problem in tech, and this has an outsized impact on the Black community. We want to invest in building out the next generation of technical talent for the industry and expanding the opportunities for underrepresented minorities. We also want to accelerate this change right now. To find the best talent for technical and non-technical roles, we actively partner with historically Black colleges and universities on our recruiting, internship, and upskilling initiatives.

Let me close by saying that I believe Amazon should be scrutinized. We should scrutinize all large institutions, whether they're companies, government agencies, or non-profits. Our responsibility is to make sure we pass such scrutiny with flying colors.

It's not a coincidence that Amazon was born in this country. More than any other place on Earth, new companies can start, grow, and thrive here in the U.S. Our country embraces resourcefulness and self-reliance, and it embraces builders who start from scratch. We nurture entrepreneurs and start-ups with stable rule of law, the finest university system in the world, the freedom of democracy, and a deeply accepted culture of risk-taking. Of course, this great nation of ours is far from perfect. Even as we remember Congressman John Lewis and honor his legacy, we're in the middle of a much-needed race reckoning. We also face the challenges of climate change and income inequality, and we're stumbling through the crisis of a global pandemic.

Still, the rest of the world would love even the tiniest sip of the elixir we have here in the U.S. Immigrants like my dad see what a treasure this country is—they have perspective and can often see it even more clearly than those of us who were lucky enough to be born here. It's still Day One for this country, and even in the face of today's humbling challenges, I have never been more optimistic about our future.

I appreciate the opportunity to appear before you today and am happy to take your questions.

Jeff Bezos steps down as Amazon CEO

Full text of the Jeff Bezos' email to Amazon employees.

Amazon founder Jeff Bezos, 57, has announced that he will be stepping down as the Chief Executive Officer (CEO) of the e-commerce giant later this year, handing over the reins of the company to Andy Jassy. In a memo addressing all Amazon employees, Bezos said this move would allow him "the time and energy I need to focus on the Day1 Fund, the Bezos Earth Fund, Blue Origin, *The Washington Post*, and my other passions".

Fellow Amazonians,

"I am excited to announce that this Q3 I'll transition to Executive Chair of the Amazon Board and Andy Jassy will become CEO. In the Exec Chair role, I intend to focus my energies and attention on new products and early initiatives. Andy is well known inside the company and has been at Amazon almost as long as I have. He will be an outstanding leader, and he has my full confidence.

This journey began some 27 years ago. Amazon was only an idea, and it had no name. The question I was asked most frequently at that time was, "What's the internet?" Blessedly, I have not had to explain that in a long while. Today, we employ 1.3 million talented, dedicated people, serve hundreds of millions of customers and businesses, and are widely recognized as one of the most successful companies in the world.

How did that happen? Invention. Invention is the root of our success. We have done crazy things together, and then made them normal. We pioneered customer reviews, 1-Click, personalized recommendations, Prime's insanely-fast shipping, Just Walk Out shopping, the Climate Pledge, Kindle, Alexa, marketplace, infrastructure cloud computing, Career Choice, and much more. If you get it right, a few years after a surprising invention, the new thing has become normal. People yawn. And that yawn is the greatest compliment an inventor can receive.

I do not know of another company with an invention track record as good as Amazon's, and I believe we are at our most inventive right now. I hope you are as proud of our inventiveness as I am. I think you should be.

As Amazon became large, we decided to use our scale and scope to lead on important social issues. Two high-impact examples: our $15 minimum wage and the Climate Pledge. In both cases, we staked out leadership positions and then asked others to come along with us. In both cases, it is working. Other large companies are coming our way. I hope you are proud of that as well.

I find my work meaningful and fun. I get to work with the smartest, most talented, most ingenious teammates. When times have been good, you have been humble. When times have been tough, you have been strong and supportive, and we have made each other laugh. It is a joy to work on this team.

As much as I still tap dance into the office, I am excited about this transition. Millions of customers depend on us for our services, and more than a million employees depend on us for their livelihoods. Being the CEO of Amazon is a deep responsibility, and it is consuming. When you have a responsibility like that, it is hard to put attention on anything else. As Exec Chair I will stay engaged in important Amazon initiatives but also have the time and energy I need to focus on the Day 1 Fund, the Bezos Earth Fund, Blue Origin, The Washington Post, and my other passions. I have never had more energy, and this is not about retiring. I am super passionate about the impact I think these organizations can have.

Amazon could not be better positioned for the future. We are firing on all cylinders, just as the world needs us to. We have things in the pipeline that will continue to astonish. We serve individuals and enterprises, and we have pioneered two complete industries and a whole new class of devices. We are leaders in areas as varied as machine learning and logistics, and if an Amazonian's idea requires yet another new institutional skill, we are flexible enough and patient enough to learn it.

Keep inventing, and do not despair when at first the idea looks crazy. Remember to wander. Let curiosity be your compass. It remains Day 1. -- Jeff

Final letter to shareholders

Before turning the helm to Andy Jassy

In Amazon's 1997 letter to shareholders, our first, I talked about our hope to create an "enduring franchise," one that would reinvent what it means to serve customers by unlocking the internet's power. I noted that Amazon had grown from having 158 employees to 614, and that we had surpassed 1.5 million customer accounts. We had just gone public at a split-adjusted stock price of $1.50 per share.
I wrote that it was Day 1.

We've come a long way since then, and we are working harder than ever to serve and delight customers. Last year, we hired 500,000 employees and now directly employ 1.3 million people around the world. We have more than 200 million Prime members worldwide. More than 1.9 million small and medium-sized businesses sell in our store, and they make up close to 60% of our retail sales. Customers have connected more than 100 million smart home devices to Alexa. Amazon Web Services serves millions of customers and ended 2020 with a $50 billion annualized run rate. In 1997, we hadn't invented Prime, Marketplace, Alexa, or AWS. They weren't even ideas then, and none was preordained. We took great risk with each one and put sweat and ingenuity into each one. Along the way, we've created $1.6 trillion of wealth for shareowners. Who are they? Your Chair is one, and my Amazon shares have made me wealthy. But more than 7/8ths of the shares, representing $1.4 trillion of wealth creation, are owned by others. Who are they? They're pension funds, universities, and 401(k)s, and they're Mary and Larry, who sent me this note out of the blue just as I was sitting down to write this shareholder letter:

I am approached with similar stories all the time. I know people who've used their Amazon money for college, for emergencies, for houses, for vacations, to start their own business, for charity – and the list goes on. I'm proud of the wealth we've created for shareowners. It's significant, and it improves their lives. But I also know something else: it's not the largest part of the value we've created.

Create More Than You Consume

If you want to be successful in business (in life, actually), you have to create more than you consume. Your goal should be to create value for everyone you interact with. Any business that doesn't create value for those it touches, even if it appears successful on the surface, isn't long for this world. It's on the way out.

Remember that stock prices are not about the past. They are a prediction of future cash flows discounted back to the present. The stock market anticipates. I'm going to switch gears for a moment and talk about the past. How much value did we create for shareowners in 2020? This is a relatively easy question to answer because accounting systems are set up to answer it. Our net income in 2020 was $21.3 billion. If, instead of being a publicly traded company with thousands of owners,

Amazon were a sole proprietorship with a single owner, that's how much the owner would have earned in 2020.
How about employees? This is also a reasonably easy value creation question to answer because we can look at compensation expense. What is an expense for a company is income for employees. In 2020, employees earned $80 billion, plus another $11 billion to include benefits and various payroll taxes, for a total of $91 billion.
How about third-party sellers? We have an internal team (the Selling Partner Services team) that works to answer that question. They estimate that, in 2020, third-party seller profits from selling on Amazon were between $25 billion and $39 billion, and to be conservative here I'll go with $25 billion.

For customers, we have to break it down into consumer customers and AWS customers.
We'll do consumers first. We offer low prices, vast selection, and fast delivery, but imagine we ignore all of that for the purpose of this estimate and value only one thing: we save customers time.
Customers complete 28% of purchases on Amazon in three minutes or less, and half of all purchases are finished in less than 15 minutes. Compare that to the typical shopping trip to a physical store – driving, parking, searching store aisles, waiting in the checkout line, finding your car, and driving home. Research suggests the typical physical store trip takes about an hour. If you assume that a typical Amazon purchase takes 15 minutes and that it saves you a couple of trips to a

physical store a week, that's more than 75 hours a year saved. That's important. We're all busy in the early 21st century.

So that we can get a dollar figure, let's value the time savings at $10 per hour, which is conservative. Seventy-five hours multiplied by $10 an hour and subtracting the cost of Prime gives you value creation for each Prime member of about $630. We have 200 million Prime members, for a total in 2020 of $126 billion of value creation.

AWS is challenging to estimate because each customer's workload is so different, but we'll do it anyway, acknowledging up front that the error bars are high. Direct cost improvements from operating in the cloud versus on premises vary, but a reasonable estimate is 30%. Across AWS's entire 2020 revenue of $45 billion, that 30% would imply customer value creation of $19 billion (what would have cost them $64 billion on their own cost $45 billion from AWS). The difficult part of this estimation exercise is that the direct cost reduction is the smallest portion of the customer benefit of moving to the cloud. The bigger benefit is the increased speed of software development – something that can significantly improve the customer's competitiveness and top line. We have no reasonable way of estimating that portion of customer value except to say that it's almost certainly larger than the direct cost savings. To be conservative here (and remembering we're really only trying to get ballpark

estimates), I'll say it's the same and call AWS customer value creation $38 billion in 2020.
Adding AWS and consumer together gives us total customer value creation in 2020 of $164 billion.
Summarizing:
Shareholders: $21B
Employees: $91B
3P-Sellers:$25B
Customers $164B
Total: $301B

If each group had an income statement representing their interactions with Amazon, the numbers above would be the "bottom lines" from those income statements. These numbers are part of the reason why people work for us, why sellers sell through us, and why customers buy from us. We create value for them. And this value creation is not a zero-sum game. It is not just moving money from one pocket to another. Draw the box big around all of society, and you'll find that invention is the root of all real value creation. And value created is best thought of as a metric for innovation.

Of course, our relationship with these constituencies and the value we create isn't exclusively dollars and cents. Money doesn't tell the whole story. Our relationship with shareholders, for example, is relatively simple. They invest and hold shares for a duration of their choosing. We provide direction to shareowners infrequently on matters such as annual meetings and the right process to vote their shares. And even then they can ignore those directions and just skip voting.

Our relationship with employees is a very different example. We have processes they follow and standards they meet. We require training and various certifications. Employees have to show up at appointed times. Our interactions with employees are many, and they're fine-grained. It's not just about the pay and the benefits. It's about all the other detailed aspects of the relationship too.
Does your Chair take comfort in the outcome of the recent union vote in Bessemer? No, he doesn't. I think we need to do a better job for our employees. While the voting results were lopsided and our direct relationship with employees is strong, it's clear to me that we need a better vision for how we create value for employees – a vision for their success.

If you read some of the news reports, you might think we have no care for employees. In those reports, our employees are sometimes accused of being desperate souls and treated as robots. That's not accurate. They're sophisticated and thoughtful people who have options for where to work. When we survey fulfillment center employees, 94% say they would recommend Amazon to a friend as a place to work.
Employees are able to take informal breaks throughout their shifts to stretch, get water, use the rest room, or talk to a manager, all without impacting their performance. These

informal work breaks are in addition to the 30-minute lunch and 30-minute break built into their normal schedule.

We don't set unreasonable performance goals. We set achievable performance goals that take into account tenure and actual employee performance data. Performance is evaluated over a long period of time as we know that a variety of things can impact performance in any given week, day, or hour. If employees are on track to miss a performance target over a period of time, their manager talks with them and provides coaching.
Coaching is also extended to employees who are excelling and in line for increased responsibilities. In fact, 82% of coaching is positive, provided to employees who are meeting or exceeding expectations. We terminate the employment of less than 2.6% of employees due to their inability to perform their jobs (and that number was even lower in 2020 because of operational impacts of COVID-19).

Earth's Best Employer and Earth's Safest Place to Work
The fact is, the large team of thousands of people who lead operations at Amazon have always cared deeply for our hourly employees, and we're proud of the work environment we've created. We're also proud of the fact that Amazon is a company that does more than just create jobs for computer scientists and people with advanced degrees. We create jobs for people who never got that advantage.

Despite what we've accomplished, it's clear to me that we need a better vision for our employees' success. We have always wanted to be Earth's Most Customer-Centric Company. We won't change that. It's what got us here. But I am committing us to an addition. We are going to be Earth's Best Employer and Earth's Safest Place to Work.

In my upcoming role as Executive Chair, I'm going to focus on new initiatives. I'm an inventor. It's what I enjoy the most and what I do best. It's where I create the most value. I'm excited to work alongside the large team of passionate people we have in Ops and help invent in this arena of Earth's Best Employer and Earth's Safest Place to Work. On the details, we at Amazon are always flexible, but on matters of vision we are stubborn and relentless. We have never failed when we set our minds to something, and we're not going to fail at this either.

We dive deep into safety issues. For example, about 40% of work-related injuries at Amazon are related to musculoskeletal disorders (MSDs), things like sprains or strains that can be caused by repetitive motions. MSDs are common in the type of work that we do and are more likely to occur during an employee's first six months. We need to invent solutions to reduce MSDs for new employees, many of whom might be working in a physical role for the first time.
One such program is WorkingWell – which we launched to 859,000 employees at 350 sites across North America and

Europe in 2020 – where we coach small groups of employees on body mechanics, proactive wellness, and safety. In addition to reducing workplace injuries, these concepts have a positive impact on regular day-to-day activities outside work.

We're developing new automated staffing schedules that use sophisticated algorithms to rotate employees among jobs that use different muscle-tendon groups to decrease repetitive motion and help protect employees from MSD risks. This new technology is central to a job rotation program that we're rolling out throughout 2021.
Our increased attention to early MSD prevention is already achieving results. From 2019 to 2020, overall MSDs decreased by 32%, and MSDs resulting in time away from work decreased by more than half.

We employ 6,200 safety professionals at Amazon. They use the science of safety to solve complex problems and establish new industry best practices. In 2021, we'll invest more than $300 million into safety projects, including an initial $66 million to create technology that will help prevent collisions of forklifts and other types of industrial vehicles.

When we lead, others follow. Two and a half years ago, when we set a $15 minimum wage for our hourly employees, we did so because we wanted to lead on wages – not just run with the pack – and because we believed it was the right thing to do. A recent paper by economists at the University of

California-Berkeley and Brandeis University analyzed the impact of our decision to raise our minimum starting pay to $15 per hour. Their assessment reflects what we've heard from employees, their families, and the communities they live in.

Our increase in starting wage boosted local economies across the country by benefiting not only our own employees but also other workers in the same community. The study showed that our pay raise resulted in a 4.7% increase in the average hourly wage among other employers in the same labor market.
And we're not done leading. If we want to be Earth's Best Employer, we shouldn't settle for 94% of employees saying they would recommend Amazon to a friend as a place to work. We have to aim for 100%. And we'll do that by continuing to lead on wages, on benefits, on upskilling opportunities, and in other ways that we will figure out over time.

If any shareowners are concerned that Earth's Best Employer and Earth's Safest Place to Work might dilute our focus on Earth's Most Customer-Centric Company, let me set your mind at ease. Think of it this way. If we can operate two businesses as different as consumer ecommerce and AWS, and do both at the highest level, we can certainly do the same with these two vision statements. In fact, I'm confident they will reinforce each other.

The Climate Pledge

In an earlier draft of this letter, I started this section with arguments and examples designed to demonstrate that human-induced climate change is real. But, bluntly, I think we can stop saying that now. You don't have to say that photosynthesis is real, or make the case that gravity is real, or that water boils at 100 degrees Celsius at sea level. These things are simply true, as is the reality of climate change.

Not long ago, most people believed that it would be good to address climate change, but they also thought it would cost a lot and would threaten jobs, competitiveness, and economic growth. We now know better. Smart action on climate change will not only stop bad things from happening, it will also make our economy more efficient, help drive technological change, and reduce risks. Combined, these can lead to more and better jobs, healthier and happier children, more productive workers, and a more prosperous future. This doesn't mean it will be easy. It won't be. The coming decade will be decisive. The economy in 2030 will need to be vastly different from what it is today, and Amazon plans to be at the heart of the change. We launched The Climate Pledge together with Global Optimism in September 2019 because we wanted to help drive this positive revolution. We need to be part of a growing team of corporations that understand the imperatives and the opportunities of the 21st century.

Now, less than two years later, 53 companies representing almost every sector of the economy have signed The Climate Pledge. Signatories such as Best Buy, IBM, Infosys, Mercedes-Benz, Microsoft, Siemens, and Verizon have committed to achieve net-zero carbon in their worldwide businesses by 2040, 10 years ahead of the Paris Agreement. The Pledge also requires them to measure and report greenhouse gas emissions on a regular basis; implement decarbonization strategies through real business changes and innovations; and neutralize any remaining emissions with additional, quantifiable, real, permanent, and socially beneficial offsets. Credible, quality offsets are precious, and we should reserve them to compensate for economic activities where low-carbon alternatives don't exist.

The Climate Pledge signatories are making meaningful, tangible, and ambitious commitments. Uber has a goal of operating as a zero-emission platform in Canada, Europe, and the U.S. by 2030, and Henkel plans to source 100% of the electricity it uses for production from renewable sources. Amazon is making progress toward our own goal of 100% renewable energy by 2025, five years ahead of our initial 2030 target. Amazon is the largest corporate buyer of renewable energy in the world. We have 62 utility-scale wind and solar projects and 125 solar rooftops on fulfillment and sort centers around the globe. These projects have the capacity to generate over 6.9 gigawatts and deliver more than 20 million megawatt-hours of energy annually.

Transportation is a major component of Amazon's business operations and the toughest part of our plan to meet net-zero carbon by 2040. To help rapidly accelerate the market for electric vehicle technology, and to help all companies transition to greener technologies, we invested more than $1 billion in Rivian – and ordered 100,000 electric delivery vans from the company. We've also partnered with Mahindra in India and Mercedes-Benz in Europe. These custom electric delivery vehicles from Rivian are already operational, and they first hit the road in Los Angeles this past February. Ten thousand new vehicles will be on the road as early as next year, and all 100,000 vehicles will be on the road by 2030 – saving millions of metric tons of carbon. A big reason we want companies to join The Climate Pledge is to signal to the marketplace that businesses should start inventing and developing new technologies that signatories need to make good on the Pledge. Our purchase of 100,000 Rivian electric vans is a perfect example.

To further accelerate investment in new technologies needed to build a zero-carbon economy, we introduced the Climate Pledge Fund last June. The investment program started with $2 billion to invest in visionary companies that aim to facilitate the transition to a low-carbon economy. Amazon has already announced investments in CarbonCure Technologies, Pachama, Redwood Materials, Rivian, Turntide Technologies, ZeroAvia, and Infinium – and these are just some of the innovative companies we hope will build the zero-carbon economy of the future.

I have also personally allocated $10 billion to provide grants to help catalyze the systemic change we will need in the coming decade. We'll be supporting leading scientists, activists, NGOs, environmental justice organizations, and others working to fight climate change and protect the natural world. Late last year, I made my first round of grants to 16 organizations working on innovative and needle-moving solutions. It's going to take collective action from big companies, small companies, nation states, global organizations, and individuals, and I'm excited to be part of this journey and optimistic that humanity can come together to solve this challenge.

Differentiation is Survival and the Universe Wants You to be Typical

This is my last annual shareholder letter as the CEO of Amazon, and I have one last thing of utmost importance I feel compelled to teach. I hope all Amazonians take it to heart.

Here is a passage from Richard Dawkins' (extraordinary) book The Blind Watchmaker. It's about a basic fact of biology.

"Staving off death is a thing that you have to work at. Left to itself – and that is what it is when it dies – the body tends to revert to a state of equilibrium with its environment. If you measure some quantity such as the temperature, the acidity, the water content or the electrical potential in a living body, you will typically find that it is markedly different from the corresponding measure in the surroundings. Our bodies, for instance, are usually hotter than our surroundings, and in cold climates they have to work hard to maintain the differential. When we die the work stops, the temperature differential starts to disappear, and we end up the same temperature as our surroundings. Not all animals work so hard to avoid coming into equilibrium with their surrounding temperature, but all animals do some comparable work. For instance, in a dry country, animals and plants work to maintain the fluid content of their cells, work against a natural tendency for water to flow from them into the dry outside world. If they fail they die. More generally, if living things didn't work actively to prevent it, they would eventually merge into their surroundings, and cease to exist as autonomous beings. That is what happens when they die."

While the passage is not intended as a metaphor, it's nevertheless a fantastic one, and very relevant to Amazon. I would argue that it's relevant to all companies and all institutions and to each of our individual lives too. In what ways does the world pull at you in an attempt to make you normal? How much work does it take to maintain your distinctiveness? To keep alive the thing or things that make you special?

I know a happily married couple who have a running joke in their relationship. Not infrequently, the husband looks at the wife with faux distress and says to her, “Can’t you just be normal?” They both smile and laugh, and of course the deep truth is that her distinctiveness is something he loves about her. But, at the same time, it’s also true that things would often be easier – take less energy – if we were a little more normal.

This phenomenon happens at all scale levels. Democracies are not normal. Tyranny is the historical norm. If we stopped doing all of the continuous hard work that is needed to maintain our distinctiveness in that regard, we would quickly come into equilibrium with tyranny.

We all know that distinctiveness – originality – is valuable. We are all taught to “be yourself.” What I’m really asking you to do is to embrace and be realistic about how much energy it takes to maintain that distinctiveness. The world wants you to be typical – in a thousand ways, it pulls at you. Don’t let it happen.

You have to pay a price for your distinctiveness, and it’s worth it. The fairy tale version of “be yourself” is that all the pain stops as soon as you allow your distinctiveness to shine. That version is misleading. Being yourself is worth it, but don’t expect it to be easy or free. You’ll have to put energy into it continuously.

The world will always try to make Amazon more typical – to bring us into equilibrium with our environment. It will take continuous effort, but we can and must be better than that.

As always, I attach our 1997 shareholder letter. It concluded with this: "We at Amazon.com are grateful to our customers for their business and trust, to each other for our hard work, and to our shareholders for their support and encouragement." That hasn't changed a bit.

I want to especially thank Andy Jassy for agreeing to take on the CEO role. It's a hard job with a lot of responsibility. Andy is brilliant and has the highest of high standards. I guarantee you that Andy won't let the universe make us typical. He will muster the energy needed to keep alive in us what makes us special. That won't be easy, but it is critical. I also predict it will be satisfying and oftentimes fun. Thank you, Andy.
To all of you: be kind, be original, create more than you consume, and never, never, never let the universe smooth you into your surroundings. It remains Day 1.

Sincerely,
To our shareowners:

Jeffrey P. Bezos

Founder and Chief Executive Officer
Amazon.com, Inc

Lightning Source UK Ltd.
Milton Keynes UK
UKHW010141030821
388208UK00001B/30

9 782923 241661